LEGENDS

The Best Players, Games,
and Teams in

BASEBALL

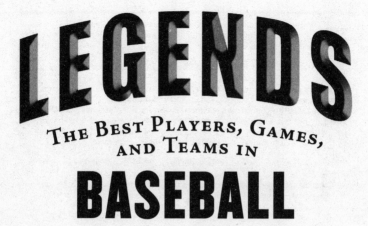

LEGENDS

THE BEST PLAYERS, GAMES, AND TEAMS IN

BASEBALL

HOWARD BRYANT

PUFFIN BOOKS

PUFFIN BOOKS
An imprint of Penguin Random House LLC
375 Hudson Street
New York, New York 10014

First published in the United States of America by Philomel Books,
an imprint of Penguin Young Readers Group, 2015
Published by Puffin Books, an imprint of Penguin Random House LLC, 2016

THE LIBRARY OF CONGRESS HAS CATALOGED THE PHILOMEL BOOKS EDITION AS FOLLOWS:
Bryant, Howard, 1968–
Legends: the best players, games, and teams in baseball / Howard Bryant.
pages cm.—(Legends; 1) Audience: Age: 8–12. Audience: Grade: 4 to 6.
ISBN 978-0-399-16903-8 (hardcover)
1. Baseball—United States—History—Juvenile literature.
2. Baseball players—United States—Biography—Juvenile literature.
I. Title. GV867.5.B79 2015
796.357′64—dc 23 2014031744

Puffin Books ISBN 978-0-14-751262-8

Printed in the United States of America

3 5 7 9 10 8 6 4 2

PHOTO CREDITS

For Ilan Robert Bryant,
a wonderful little boy who likes baseball,
but loves to read

CONTENTS

A Note from Howard Bryant

THIS IS NOT A PERFECT BOOK. The best thing you, the reader, can do with it is disagree with it, debate it, change it, have fun with it, decide for yourself that THE 2010-2014 San Francisco Giants WHO WON THREE WORLD SERIES IN FIVE YEARS, are ABSOLUTELY a dynasty on par with the 1996-2001 New York Yankees, who won four World Series in six years (I would argue otherwise). Countless hours of your life are going to be spent debating stuff like which team was better, the 2013 Red Sox with their beards and that strange way they didn't seem to be that good and yet always found a way to win, found a way to be great at just the right time right through the World Series; or the 2000 Yankees, who finished the regular season so bad they couldn't even win two games in a row—until the playoffs started and then they got red hot, trampling the A's, the Mariners, and the Mets to win the World Series for the third straight year. When you and your friends disagree, you can grab the *Baseball Encyclopedia* or get on baseball-reference.com and look up the stats and tell them they're nuts to think that there was ever anyone better when it came to making a big play when a big play needed to be made than Derek Jeter, and they'll say that David Ortiz was the most clutch hitter there ever was. And another friend will say, "Obviously, you're forgetting Babe Ruth, who invented the word *clutch*." And maybe someone else will say, "You know, for as great as Ruth was, he DID make one of the biggest boneheaded plays you could make. He got thrown out trying to steal second in Game Seven of the 1926 World Series. True story!" (And it is, for even the greatest players make mistakes, too.) When you look back one day, you'll remember those debates as some of the best times of your life.

Baseball has been around so long that, no matter how hard anyone tries, there is no such thing as a perfect list. It just can't be done. The first World Series was played in 1903 between Boston and Pittsburgh, but baseball was being played thirty years before that—which was so long ago that the guys were hitting home runs and striking out less than ten years after the Civil War—and more than one hundred years after, to this day. The game has lived through twenty-six presidents and is now in its third century. It was played when the ball felt like a boulder (the old "dead ball" era, when a guy named Home Run Baker led the league with, yes, NINE homers); when it took *eight* balls for a batter to earn a walk (they changed it to four in 1889); and when pitchers threw underhand, like they do in softball. (That changed in 1884.) There was a time when none of the baseball parks had lights. The Reds played the first-ever night game in 1935, but the Cubs didn't play their first home night game until 1988. White men were once the only players allowed to play. Jackie Robinson and Roberto Clemente and Ichiro Suzuki changed history, and during that time great players did amazing things that people still talk about to this day, just as things are happening now on the field that people will talk about far into the future.

So who gets to decide what players, games, and teams are the best of all time? You do. This is just a road map to get you started, to go back into history through the years before television, before there were teams in San Francisco or Los Angeles or Seattle, and to add those long-lost teams and feats and deeds to the amazing plays being made in baseball today. The great players of today, like Mike Trout or Justin Verlander or Clayton Kershaw, compared to the likes of Babe Ruth and Willie Mays and Hank Aaron.

In the end, whether in 1914 or 2014, the game always finishes in the same way, with a group of happy ballplayers being the only team in the league to win the last game of the season, pouring champagne over each other's heads.

What matters is what the sport means to you. When I first started reading about baseball, Bob Gibson, Sandy Koufax, Willie Mays, and Jackie Robinson became my favorite players even though I had never seen any of them play in person. I went outside, played second base, and thought I was Robinson, dirt under my feet, ready to steal second and, if the ball got by, ready to get up and take third—even though he retired twelve years before I was even born. How is that possible? He was that good, and at the end of this journey, hopefully you'll do what this book is intended for you to do: Make your own lists; learn about and imagine the people who built the game of baseball and the moments and players who are building it now. After 150 years, baseball is still a fantastic trip worth taking.

The One and Only

BABE RUTH

T here are certain figures in American history whose names, no matter how long ago they lived, are timeless. They remain even as time moves forward. Most are either presidents or businessmen whose companies or foundations still exist with their famous names. But there are few entertainers and athletes whose names have survived an entire century, long after their time has passed.

In baseball, there is one above everyone else, and his name is Babe Ruth.

There have been many great players over the history of baseball. Joe DiMaggio, Ted Williams, Willie

Mays, Henry Aaron, Ty Cobb. Why was Ruth so much bigger than everyone else? Why is he still such a memorable figure to this day? Ruth was born in 1895, played his last game in 1935, and died in 1948— yet people still talk about him.

There are many reasons, and all of them are important. The first is that he was the player who made baseball what it is today. Before Ruth, hits were more important than home runs. Before Ruth, New York was just another place to play, a city overshadowed in importance by more successful baseball cities like Chicago and Boston. Before Ruth, baseball was a popular sport. With Ruth, it became not only the most popular sport in America, but the national pastime.

Growing up, Ruth did not seem to have much of a chance to survive, never mind become the most famous baseball player of all time, and one of the most popular Americans in history. He was born poor and without a family. He was raised in an orphanage in Baltimore. He was always in trouble and was constantly caught by the police for skipping school. Ruth had very little going for him, but he somehow found himself in New York, as America's most famous ballplayer in America's most famous city.

All of the odds were against him, and yet he made the American dream happen.

Ruth had oversized talent and a huge personality. He was big. He grew to be six-foot-two and weighed 215 pounds. He was funny and he laughed and joked with everyone. He boasted he could eat twenty hot dogs in one sitting. He drove people crazy doing things his own way, but he was so good he got away with a lot. Ruth made everyone around him (except people in authority, like his managers) feel good—always the life of the party. He was the kid in class who was popular and good at sports but was never mean to anyone else. He made the younger kids, the less popular kids, all feel special. For that, people loved him.

"The Babe" was larger than life. He was like a comic book, a figment of a kid's imagination—except that he was real. He was bigger and better than everyone else who stepped on a ball field. When he arrived in Boston as a rookie in 1914, he was already one of the best pitchers in baseball, *and then* he became the best hitter. Who else does that? For years, baseball was played with a ball that felt like lead. It was heavy and weighted in the center, which made it difficult to hit home runs. That period was called the "dead-ball era." During part of that time, Ruth pitched as a member of the Boston Red Sox, and he dominated. He was a great pitcher, leading the Red Sox to the World Series in 1915, 1916, and 1918.

In 1920, the year the Red Sox sold Ruth to the Yankees, baseball leagues began using a ball that had a light cork in the center. When it was hit, the new ball flew longer and farther than the dead ball. When Ruth hit the ball, it traveled seemingly for miles. Fans of all ages loved it, and they came to baseball games in record numbers, in a way they never had before. A star was born, and it was during the 1920s, when Babe Ruth was at his peak, that baseball became America's national pastime. He stopped pitching and became the greatest power hitter the game had ever seen.

Before Ruth, no one had ever hit 20 home runs in a season. In New York, he hit 54 homers in his first year, and 59 in his second. From 1926 to 1931 he led the league in home runs each year. He played 22 seasons and led the majors in home runs 11 times!

With Ruth, it wasn't just home runs, but the dominance of his offensive game. He won a batting title in 1924 when he hit .378. He led the league in runs scored eight times. He led the league in runs batted in five times. He was so good no one wanted to pitch to him and while crushing pitchers everywhere, he still led the league in walks 11 times. He hasn't played a game in 80 years and still is the career leader in three more categories!

And this was all happening just as the film industry was taking off, just when people started going to the movies. Game highlights on ESPN are normal by today's standards, but back then Ruth was the first sports film star in America, the first to be embraced by the entire nation rather than just a city. Most fans didn't get to go to ball games, so they listened on the radio or read about their favorites in the newspaper. In their imaginations, all kids across America wanted to be Babe Ruth.

Ruth became a star in New York. People came to see the big man hit. They came to see him swing and hit home runs. They came to see him swing and miss. They loved how big his personality was, how many nicknames he had. He was the Babe. He was the Bambino. He was the Sultan of Swat. Even his strikeouts were dramatic. Sometimes, Ruth swung so hard he fell down. No one in the history of baseball had ever been such a showman and a salesman for the game. Though the company would consistently deny it, most people believed they even named a candy bar after him—Baby Ruth! (For the record, the candy company claimed the bar was named after President Grover Cleveland's daughter, Ruth Cleveland, though nobody really believed them.)

There was something else about Ruth. He wasn't just the greatest player in the biggest city in America—he was a game changer. He was a winner. When Ruth arrived, the Yankees went from losers to winners. Ruth liked to do things big, and it was no coincidence that with him the Yankees became the biggest winners in the history of baseball, a title they still own to this day. Before Ruth, the Yankees had *never* appeared in the World Series. In 1921, his second year in New York, the Yankees went to the World Series for the first time, even though they lost. They went again—and lost—in 1922.

Yet Ruth's popularity was making the Yankees so rich that the owner, Col. Jacob Ruppert, built a new ballpark for the team. It was called Yankee Stadium and it opened in 1923. The stadium was enormous, except for one place: right field. The fences in right were among the shortest in baseball, designed specifically for Ruth, who hit left-handed, to have the best chance at hitting all those home runs.

Today, it is often known as the "House that Ruth Built" to honor the man whose greatness stands eternal.

Ruth's Yankees changed American sports. The first year in their new ballpark, 1923, they won their first World Series. There were great teams in the past, like John McGraw's New York Giants, but the Yankees reached a new level of dominance. They won the series again in 1927 and 1928. Then, after a three-year absence, the Yankees returned to the World Series in 1932 against the Chicago Cubs. The Yankees swept that series in four games, but that's not what people remember. To this day, people still talk about Game 3, when Ruth pointed his bat toward the center field bleachers, as if to tell the pitcher where his hit was going to land. On the very next pitch, he slammed one out of the park, into the center field bleachers. Ruth was so good he had even called his own shot.

For generations, Babe Ruth was the greatest home run hitter who ever lived. His single-season record of 60 home runs was thought to be unreachable and stood for 34 years. He hit 714 home runs over his 22-year career, which was another number no one ever thought could be broken. It was a record that stood for 39 years. They were the two most celebrated and chased-after records in baseball.

When Ruth retired, nearly every offensive record in the book—and even some pitching ones—belonged to him. He won the World Series three times with the Red Sox and four more times with the Yankees. Ruth was the model for the modern superstar. People still talk about him, because he was Michael Jordan, Peyton Manning, Kobe Bryant, and Tom Brady combined. He talked big and played even bigger—in doing so, he became the idol of baseball fans across America. And to this day, he's still an idol—for not a single baseball fan, alive or dead, hasn't heard of the greatness of Babe Ruth.

TOP TEN LIST

Babe Ruth's career was defined by dominance. In particular, Ruth's home run hitting prowess allowed him to lead not just the American League, but all of Major League Baseball in home runs eleven times, the most ever by any player. Here are other players who dominated the competition during their careers:

1. Barry Bonds: Most MVP awards—7 (1990, 1992–1993, 2001–2004)
2. Roger Clemens: Most Cy Young awards—7 (1986–1987, 1991, 1997–1998, 2001, 2004)
3. Brooks Robinson / Jim Kaat: Most consecutive seasons winning a Gold Glove award—16 (Robinson: 1960–1975; Kaat: 1962–1977)
4. Ty Cobb: Most seasons leading the majors in batting average—11 (or 10*) (1907, 1909–1915, 1917–1919 [tied 1907])
5. Walter Johnson / Randy Johnson: Most seasons

leading the majors in strikeouts by a pitcher—8 (W. Johnson: 1910, 1912–1914, 1916, 1918–1919, 1921; R. Johnson: 1993–1995, 1999, 2000–2002, 2004)

6. Alex Rodriguez: Most seasons with 100+ runs batted in—14 (1996, 1998–2010)

7. Lou Brock / Rickey Henderson: Most seasons leading the majors in stolen bases—6 (Brock: 1966, 1968, 1971–1974; Henderson: 1980, 1982–1983, 1988–1989, 1998)

8. Cy Young (yes, the award was named after him): Most seasons with 20+ wins for a pitcher—15 (1891–1899, 1901–1904, 1907–1908)

9. Ty Cobb / Pete Rose / Ichiro Suzuki: Most seasons leading the majors in hits—7 (Cobb: 1907, 1909, 1911–1912, 1915, 1917, 1919 [tied in 1912, 1919]; Rose: 1965, 1968, 1970, 1972–1973, 1976, 1981 [tied in 1968, 1970, 1976]; Suzuki: 2001, 2004, 2006–2010 [tied in 2008])

10. Nolan Ryan: Most career no-hitters—7 (1973, 1973, 1974, 1975, 1981, 1990, 1991)

*Different sources dispute whether Ty Cobb or Nap Lajoie won the batting title in 1910

42

JACKIE ROBINSON BECOMES A LEGEND

n January 31, 1949, Jackie Robinson turned thirty. He was already famous, having been the first African American to play in the major leagues during the modern era two years earlier in 1947. For that, the history books would always remember him. In that first year, he was named the National League Rookie of the Year, and his team, the Brooklyn Dodgers, made it to the World Series, losing to the New York Yankees in seven difficult games. Robinson had already proven a great deal that

first year. He proved blacks and whites could compete on the same field peacefully, which in 1947 many people—including many of his teammates—did not think possible. He proved he was strong enough to handle the responsibility of being the person who was going to change society.

And, on the baseball diamond, he proved he was a superstar.

Being a superstar means more than just putting up good statistics. Robinson played the game in a way that made kids and adults alike identify with him. He played with style. The fans loved his movements and would try to stand as he did, stationary at the plate, completely upright, the bat held high above his head, fierce and ready, waiting to strike. It was the kind of batting stance a coach would immediately try to correct, because his hands were supposedly too high, nearly even with his ear. The theory was that he wouldn't be fast enough to swing the bat through the strike zone to catch up to scorching fastballs.

For everyone else, the theory might have been right. For Jackie, it was completely wrong.

Jackie's hands were always fast enough, and when

he would bring the bat slashing down, he could drive the ball to every corner of the field: singles to right, doubles to center, and home runs to left. On the playgrounds around New York and the rest of America, fans would try to hit just like him.

When he was on base, he was even more exciting, wading slowly off first, drifting toward second, making the pitcher pay attention to him. The pitcher's job is to focus on the batter, but when Jackie was on base, he became the action. Would he steal? Was he bluffing? The pitcher would throw the ball to first, yet Jackie would easily dive back to the base in time.

Eventually the pitcher would get mad and lose his concentration. That's when Robinson would take off for second . . . or he might have proven to be such an annoyance to the pitcher that he would make a mistake and throw a hittable pitch to the batter because he'd been too busy thinking about Jackie.

Robinson would play the same mind games at third base, dancing down the line, everyone in the crowd anticipating that he would steal home. While base runners today rarely even attempt to steal home, Jackie Robinson stole home an incredible nineteen times in his career, including once in the World Series.

Jackie Robinson was simply the most exciting player in the league.

Beyond his on-field success, many fans loved him because they knew the heavy burden he was carrying by being the first African American player and how much courage it took to shoulder such responsibility. Fortunately, he wasn't the only black player for long. By 1949, two years after Robinson's debut, there were seven African American players in the major leagues. Robinson, however, remained the definitive symbol of change, both within the world of baseball and beyond.

As that symbol of change, Robinson carried different burdens, some known to the public, others not. One unknown at the time was that he had promised the Dodgers' president, Branch Rickey, that he would not fight back during his first three seasons. He promised that if an opponent or even a teammate used a bad name because of the color of his skin, he would not retaliate. He promised that if an opposing player committed a dirty play against him, such as purposely driving his spikes into Robinson's shins as he covered a base, he would not fight back. If the fans in hostile cities like Philadelphia or St. Louis called him or his family sitting in the stands names, he would not fight back. He promised to absorb all of the abuse, all of the hate that would be thrown at him, to prove that he could handle being the person who was going to change the game.

In 1949, Rickey told Robinson he had kept his promise. Rickey said to Robinson, "Jackie, you're on your own now. You can be yourself."

Free to be himself, Jackie Robinson took off, enjoying the best year of his career. He had always played the game very hard and physically, and now if someone argued with him, he didn't have to just walk away. He could argue back. "Not being able to fight back," he said, "is a form of severe punishment."

He won the batting title that season with a .342 average, led the league in stolen bases and sacrifice hits, and set personal bests in plate appearances, at-bats, hits, triples, RBIs, stolen bases, and batting average.

With Robinson at his best, his teammates followed. The Dodgers by then had two more African American players on the team: catcher Roy Campanella and pitcher Don Newcombe. Together with other Dodgers stars like Duke Snider, Gil Hodges, and Carl Furillo, the Dodgers became one of the great teams of the 1950s.

That 1949 Dodgers team won the National League pennant before losing the World Series to the Yankees in five games. The hurt of losing did not go away, but at the end of the season, Robinson was named National League Most Valuable Player for the first and only time in his career.

The legend of Jackie Robinson would continue to grow as the years went by. Over a ten-year career, he appeared in the World Series six times. A lifetime .311 hitter, he was inducted into the Hall of Fame in 1962, and would become a towering figure in history forever, far beyond his baseball achievements.

His presence would always remain large. The Rookie of the Year trophy he won in 1947 would be renamed the Jackie Robinson Award. In 1997, fifty years after Robinson entered the majors, Major League Baseball permanently retired his uniform number, 42. No new players would ever again be handed Jackie's number . . . except for one day each season, April 15, when *every* major leaguer commemorates the day one man changed the game, by wearing uniform number 42.

Jackie Robinson would forever be remembered as an American hero, but the 1949 season showed America just what a great ballplayer he was as well.

TOP TEN LIST

Robinson's entry into the major leagues in 1947 changed not only baseball, but American history. Many other players made historic contributions to baseball. Beyond Jackie Robinson, here are ten more names worth discovering.

1. Roberto Clemente: Baseball's first Latin American superstar.
2. Satchel Paige: Superstar of the Negro Leagues who, at age 42, became the oldest rookie to debut in the major leagues.
3. Babe Ruth: The first superstar in American team sports.
4. Marvin Miller: Legendary leader of the Major League Baseball Players Association.
5. Curt Flood: Outfielder who, in 1970, sacrificed his career to challenge baseball's hundred-year-old rule that players could not change teams when their contracts expired.

6. Hank Greenberg: Baseball's first Jewish superstar.

7. Branch Rickey: Legendary executive who invented the minor-league farm system and signed Jackie Robinson.

8. Larry Doby: First African American player in the American League.

9. Jim Abbott: Born with one hand, pitched in the major leagues. Threw a perfect game.

10. Toni Stone: Female infielder who played alongside men in the Negro Leagues.

Willie's Time

THE GREATNESS OF WILLIE MAYS

In the eighth inning of the first game of the 1954 World Series, Vic Wertz was ready to be a hero for the best team in baseball. His team, the Cleveland Indians, mashed everything in sight, including the Yankees, the team that had won the last five World Series in a row, and now at the Polo Grounds in New York, the Indians were about to claim Game 1 of the World Series against the New York Giants.

There were two men on base in a 2–2 game with nobody out. Wertz hit a shot to deep center field. In most stadiums, the ball would have soared into the stands, but the Polo Grounds had the deepest center field in baseball history, some 485 feet to the back wall.

The ball kept going and going. The Giants' center fielder, Willie Mays, kept running and running, 400 feet . . . 420 . . . 440. The two runners on base, Larry Doby and Al Rosen, raced for home to score the tie-breaking runs . . . Mays kept running . . . 450 feet . . . at an incredible 460 feet away, he reached out over his shoulder and caught the ball at full sprint. *Over his shoulder!*

Not only did Mays make that incredible catch, but he also remembered to turn around and throw the ball back into the infield as the runners realized they had to scramble back to their bases. Rosen scurried back to first, Doby to second. No tie-breaking runs.

In the box score, the ball Wertz hit was just another out. But in that one moment, the legend of Willie Mays was born.

Mays's catch in 1954 was more than half a century ago and is still considered the greatest catch in the history of the World Series. The old black-and-white footage of Mays running as fast as he could, seemingly hopeless before catching the ball, captures quite simply one of the greatest plays ever made on a baseball diamond—but for Mays, it was the kind of play he made all the time.

Babe Ruth may have been baseball's greatest showman at the plate. Yet Willie Mays was baseball's version of Superman. He had the power of Ruth and the speed of Jackie Robinson. He could hit for average like the great Joe DiMaggio, for example, when he hit .345 in 1954 and won the batting title, but he also had a gift in that he made throwing and catching the ball look like the most exciting parts of the game. Similar to Ruth, Mays did it all with the kind of flair that excited fans of every age, and left them wanting to play baseball just like Willie did.

Willie Mays was born May 6, 1931, in Westfield, Alabama, and was almost instantly a star baseball player. He played football in high school, but even as a pre-teen, he began playing baseball against adults. In 1949, when Mays was eighteen years old, the Boston Red Sox sent a scout to look at Mays and consider signing him. Yet the Red Sox, particularly owner Tom Yawkey, were not comfortable with having an African American player on the team. Four years earlier, the Red Sox also had chosen not to sign Jackie Robinson. Not being signed by Boston was a huge disappointment for Mays.

So Mays continued playing in all-black leagues as part of the Birmingham Black Barons. In the Negro Leagues, Mays almost immediately became the one to draw crowds to the stadium.

Eventually, the New York Giants signed Mays and assigned him to their minor league team, the Minneapolis Millers, where Mays hit .477.

Once he joined the big leagues, nothing changed—Mays set the pace. While he was a rookie in 1951, the Giants reached the World Series but lost to the Yankees. Then Mays was drafted into the US Army for two years, 1952 and 1953, spending those seasons in the military. Not coincidentally, the Giants failed to earn a shot at the pennant both seasons. But when he returned in 1954, he was spectacular—in addition to winning the batting title, he also hit 41 home runs, drove in 110 runs, led the league in triples with 13—

and made that spectacular catch in the World Series. Willie won the World Series but wasn't done, finishing off his stellar season by winning the National League Most Valuable Player Award.

For much of his 23 years in the big leagues, Willie Mays was the show, and like Ruth, everyone could tell a story about something superhuman that he'd done at one point or another. There was "The Catch," or the time in 1961 against Milwaukee when Mays hit *four home runs* in a single game. Or maybe it was the flair, the way he would catch a baseball at his waist rather than over his head—known as a basket catch. Or when he flew around the bases with the same speed he used to catch up to a fly ball.

And Willie had the coolest nickname: "The Say-Hey Kid." DiMaggio was "Jolting Joe." Henry Aaron was "Hammerin' Hank." Mickey Mantle was "The Commerce Comet," because he was from Commerce, Oklahoma, but none of those names were as easy and natural and fan-friendly as the Say Hey Kid.

When the Giants moved to San Francisco in 1958, Mays was considered the greatest player in the game—even better than Mantle or Aaron or Ernie

Banks or Frank Robinson—because he did *everything* great and had the flair to do it with style.

Yet in California, the fans of San Francisco did not love Mays immediately, because he was still considered a New York star. The fans of San Francisco were waiting to give their collective hearts to a star who had only played in San Francisco.

That finally changed in 1962. San Francisco couldn't help but adore Mays when he hit 49 home runs and drove in 141 runs, leading the Giants to their first-ever World Series after leaving New York. Not only had the Giants won the National League pennant, but they had beaten their rivals, the Dodgers. The Giants wound up playing the Yankees in the World Series that year and lost in seven hard-fought games, but baseball in San Francisco had finally been played on the big stage, and Mays was the center of attention.

It wasn't just that Mays was flashy, fun and exciting, but that he also amassed the kind of statistics that challenged the all-time great players. Mays hit 52 home runs and won another MVP Award in 1965, and it began to look like he might have a chance to catch Babe Ruth's all-time record of 714 home runs, the most celebrated record in baseball. Years of running full-speed and throwing himself into the game with everything he had caught up with him, though, and 1965 turned out to be his last great full season.

Still, there were moments when Mays would show glimmers of greatness, like in 1971 when he turned *forty years old* and led San Francisco to the playoffs. Then at age forty-two, after 22 seasons in a Giants uniform, Willie was traded back to New York, to the Mets, where he would wind up playing in one final World Series, this one against Oakland.

When his career ended after the 1973 season, his lifetime stats were unreal: .302 average, 3,283 hits, 338 stolen bases, 12 Gold Glove Awards, and 660 home runs. Yet none of the statistics ever properly described Mays. And it's not simple chance that many people have called Mays "the perfect ballplayer." To understand his greatness, you had to have seen him play. As Ted Williams once said, "They invented the All-Star Game for Willie Mays."

That pretty much says it all.

Willie Mays

TOP TEN LIST

Willie Mays was considered the perfect ballplayer—the ultimate "five-tool" player. Here are ten more players with all the tools, who could 1) run, 2) throw, 3) field, 4) hit for average, and 5) hit with power.

1. Barry Bonds, PIT-SF (1986–2007)
2. Ken Griffey Jr., SEA-CIN-CHW (1989–2009)
3. Mike Trout, LAA (2012–present)
4. Henry Aaron, MIL-ATL (NL), MIL (AL) (1954–1976)
5. Roberto Clemente, PIT (1955–1972)
6. Dave Winfield, SD-NYY-CAL-TOR-MIN-CLE (1973–1995)
7. Rickey Henderson, OAK-NYY-TOR-SD-LAA-LAD-BOS-NYM-SEA (1979–2003)
8. Mickey Mantle, NYY (1951–1968)
9. Joe DiMaggio, NYY (1936–1951)
10. Derek Jeter, NYY (1995–2014)

Too Good

~~~~~~

SIX YEARS OF
SANDY KOUFAX

Years back, when a player was so good that his statistics were practically beyond belief, others used to call him a "cartoon," meaning he could make baseball look so easy that his play resembled a cartoon, just like Bugs Bunny striking out the Crushers. Today, they call a player of the same caliber a "video game"—the kind of player who makes big-league baseball look like an Xbox game.

From 1961 to 1966, there was no better pitcher in the modern game than Sandy Koufax, the great left-hander of the Los Angeles Dodgers. Koufax was the greatest comet in the history of the game, shining bright and traveling fast across the horizon. For those six seasons, Koufax illuminated the night and just as quickly as he appeared, he was gone.

When Koufax arrived, as a nineteen-year-old, he joined the Brooklyn Dodgers, a team that played not far from where he lived. Koufax was super-talented, but he was also wild. When he pitched, no one, not even he, knew where the ball was going to go. In three years, he appeared in 62 games with Brooklyn, starting occasionally, never quite living up to the enormous future forecast for him by the organization. Koufax was just a kid, but he was expected to be a star, and in Brooklyn he was not. In 1958, the Dodgers moved to Los Angeles and Koufax was given a permanent role in the starting rotation for the first time. Everyone knew he threw hard. Everyone knew he had a fantastic curveball that looked like it was heading to the moon when it left his hand, before somehow dropping right over the plate. What no one knew was when or whether Koufax could control where the ball was going. In 1958, Koufax led the league in one statistic: wild pitches, with 17. It went this way for three more years. Even when the Dodgers won the World Series in 1959, Koufax was a talent, but not yet *great*. Certainly not a cartoon or video game.

In 1961, the moment everyone in baseball was waiting for arrived, and the results were some of the greatest performances ever seen. Koufax learned to control his white-hot fastball. He learned to control the big curveball. In 1961, he became Sandy Koufax. He won 18 games and struck out 269 hitters in only 255 2/3 innings, leading the league.

The next year, fighting injury, Koufax led the league with a 2.54 earned run average. In 1963, he won the Most Valuable Player *and* the Cy Young Awards, going 25–5 with 306 strikeouts and a 1.88 ERA. The Dodgers won the World Series, beating the hated Yankees in a four-game sweep.

In 1964, Koufax was incredible again, 19–5 with a 1.74 ERA. And he accomplished those numbers in an era of great hitters, facing Willie Mays, Frank Robinson, Roberto Clemente, Ernie Banks, and Henry Aaron. Koufax regularly faced some of the greatest hitters of all time—and he blew them all away.

Yet for all of his pitching, all of the championships and the no-hitters, being a person of substance and conscience is what separated Koufax from the rest of the pack.

In old-time baseball, pitchers and hitters engaged in an unspoken deal. The pitcher could throw at one part of the plate and the hitters could swing at the other. If a hitter tried to be too aggressive and swung too hard at both inside and outside pitches, the pitcher would immediately throw at the hitter to hit him or knock him down as a reminder not to break the un-written rules.

From the 1900s through the 1970s, pitchers were well-known for hitting batters. Bob Feller, the great Cleveland Indians fastballer, would put a hitter on his butt in a heartbeat. So would Bob Gibson and Koufax's teammate Don Drysdale. All were legendary headhunters.

Koufax threw as hard as all of them, maybe harder. He had control problems early in his career that kept him from being great, and yet Koufax was always known as a gentleman on the mound. He didn't throw at hitters. He proved that a pitcher didn't have to play mean or dirty to control the game, and that gained him the respect of players throughout baseball.

Off the field, Koufax was true to his Jewish faith. There had been several Jewish players in baseball in the past—especially during the pre–World War II years—who had suffered serious discrimination and hardship. Hank Greenberg, the great Detroit Tigers slugger, endured anti-Semitism throughout his major league career. Like in the rest of society, several Jewish players had shortened or changed their names to more "American-sounding" names to avoid the ruthless discrimination that Jews faced.

Yet Koufax was proud of his heritage. He did not hide from it. He did not shrink from his responsibilities. At first, Koufax was not obvious about his religious observance, but in 1965, when Yom Kippur, the holiest day on the Jewish calendar, fell on the opener of the World Series against the Minnesota Twins, Koufax refused to pitch. Yom Kippur represented the Day of Atonement.

To Koufax, the gesture was not a big deal, but its symbolism to Jewish fans around the country was enormous. Koufax became an even greater inspiration. He became hero to fans for more than just being a ballplayer. Generations of Jewish fans and future baseball players placed Sandy far above the rest as a favorite.

Always, with Koufax, there was great performance on the field, too. In his second start of the series, Koufax won Game 5 of the 1965 World Series 7–0, pitching the entire game and striking out 10 batters to give the Dodgers a 3–2 lead in the series. The Twins won Game 6 and so Koufax pitched for a third time, on only two days' rest, and pitched the whole game again, a complete game, 2–0 shutout to win the World Series. Two consecutive complete-game shutouts, only two days apart. Such a feat would never happen in today's game, when pitching complete games is a rarity altogether and starting pitchers struggle with as little as three days' rest between games.

Entering the 1966 season, Koufax experienced severe pain in his left elbow. Often, after pitching, the pain was so great that he could not straighten his arm. A drug new to the 1960s, cortisone, eased some of the hurt, but left Sandy feeling uncomfortable. In later years, players and team physicians would use cortisone shots routinely (though sparingly), but in 1966 its future effects were unknown and Koufax did not want to risk his health to play baseball.

Despite the pain he had to endure, Koufax pitched brilliantly that year. His arm hurt every time out, but he still pitched more innings (323) than any other pitcher in baseball, led the league with 27 wins, and only lost 9. He also led the league with 41 starts, an ERA of 1.73, and a whopping 27 complete games. To put that last statistic into context, Adam Wainwright of the Cardinals led the major leagues in complete games in 2013 . . . with *five*.

The Dodgers won the pennant again in 1966, and then faced the young, talented Baltimore Orioles in the World Series. Koufax pitched well, but the series was over in a flash: the Orioles swept the series, shutting out the Dodgers in three of the four games.

Yet the worst news for the Dodgers wasn't losing the World Series. The worst news came weeks later. At age thirty, Sandy Koufax announced he was retiring from baseball.

The pain had been too great, he said. He didn't like taking all of those shots and didn't like how the drugs made him feel.

Sandy Koufax was the best pitcher in the world at the height of his talent and he walked away from the game because he thought it would help him lead a healthier, longer life.

Baseball lost its shining comet, yet the legend of Sandy Koufax lives to this day. There have been other great pitchers who dominated for a period of years, like Greg Maddux and Pedro Martinez and Roger Clemens, but no pitcher combined three important ingredients—great pitching in the regular season, great pitching in the World Series, and inspiration as a person off the field—like Sandy Koufax.

Sandy Koufax

TOP TEN LIST

Sandy Koufax threw four no-hitters. From 1961–1966, he put up six of the greatest seasons in history, winning two World Series titles as well, with the Los Angeles Dodgers. Who are the greatest pitchers of all time? That's a discussion you could have for hours and still not agree. Here are ten names to start with, though, along with their career win totals. Note that "greatest" doesn't necessarily mean having the most wins.

1. Bob Gibson, STL (1957–1975)—251
2. Walter Johnson, WSH (1907–1927)—417
3. Tom Seaver, NYM, CIN, CHW, BOS (1967–1986)—311
4. Greg Maddux, CHC, ATL, LAD, SD (1986–2008)—355
5. Nolan Ryan, NYM, LAA, HOU, TEX (1966–1993)—324
6. Pedro Martinez, LAD, MON, BOS, NYM, PHI (1992–2009)—219

7. Warren Spahn, MIL-NYM-SFG (1942–1965)—363

8. Cy Young, CLE-STL (NL), BOS (AL), CLE (AL), BOS (NL) (1890–1911)—511

9. Randy Johnson, MON-SEA-HOU-ARI-NYY-SFG (1988–2009)—303

10. Christy Mathewson, NYG-CIN (1900–1916)—373

"Something for Me, Mama"

Henry Aaron Hits #715

Sometimes, in the middle of the night, Estella Aaron would hear the drums outside her home in Toulminville, a small town near Mobile, Alabama. The drumbeat would grow closer. She would hear footsteps. She would look out the window and see the men dressed in white robes, wearing hoods, and carrying torches.

She immediately knew who the men were. It was the Ku Klux Klan, the worst terrorist organization in America. It was the 1940s and the Klan targeted Catholics, Jews, and especially African Americans, intent on scaring them and often killing the ones who did not fear them, to keep them in their place, to remind them that they were not true Americans, that they were inferior to white Protestants. On the nights she was alone and the Klan was near, Estella would pull her eight children from their sleep and hide them under the bed to keep them safe until the danger left.

In the daytime, one of Estella Aaron's children, Henry, would hold a broomstick and try to hit bottle caps through the air. Oftentimes a friend would pitch the bottle caps to Henry and they would fly toward him, swerving and darting unpredictably, and Henry Aaron, head still, eyes focused, would easily swat the flat little crowns as though they were as big as basketballs. It was a great skill, and Henry would tell his father, Herbert, that he wanted to be a ballplayer when he grew up. "You can't," Herbert told him. "There are no colored ballplayers." Young Henry would see an airplane fly overhead, change his mind, and say, "Well, I want to be a pilot."

"You can't," Herbert Aaron told his son. "There are no colored pilots, either."

So on the playground and in his dreams, Henry stuck to baseball, hitting rocks and bottle caps and—finally—baseballs, with his friends at Carver Park. No one knew it at the time, but that kid would eventually grow into the greatest home run hitter in the history of Major League Baseball.

When Henry was fourteen he met Jackie Robinson, who had joined the Brooklyn Dodgers in 1947, and Henry's father no longer needed to tell his son he couldn't be a professional baseball player. Robinson told young Henry to work hard in school first and then concentrate on being a great baseball player. Henry smiled and agreed, but he didn't listen. He put baseball above everything, above school, above work. It paid off for him. He became one of the most famous baseball players of all time, joining the Milwaukee Braves in 1954, winning his first batting title in 1956, playing in two World Series, and winning one in 1957.

While he earned his place in baseball history by hitting home runs, Henry could do anything on the baseball diamond. He was a 21-time all-star (21 times!), won three Gold Gloves, and set records at the time for the most RBIs, extra-base hits, and total bases.

Even though he was a confident player, Henry had, in his own way, always felt overshadowed within the world of baseball. He was a great hitter, but Willie Mays was flashier. He was a solid right fielder, but everyone in baseball raved about the rocket arm of Roberto Clemente. Mickey Mantle was with the mighty Yankees and he played in New York, the big media capital. Most of all, Henry was always aware, perhaps a bit more than others in the game, of how differently society treated people based on the color of their skin.

But by the middle to late 1960s, it was clear that for all the big names, for all the guys who received more attention than he, it was Hank Aaron, and not Mantle or Mays or anyone else, who suddenly had the best chance to capture the greatest record in baseball: the all-time home run record.

The all-time home run record was the one record that no one thought would ever be broken. It belonged to Babe Ruth since his last home run, in 1935, gave him a total of 714 for his career. It was the magic number in baseball, the number all great players wanted to reach, but none ever could.

As fans and sportswriters began doing the math, it was clear that Aaron had a great shot to break the record. He was already the first player in major league history to both hit five hundred home runs and amass three thousand hits.

In 1968, the letters from the public began to arrive. Most of the letters were from fans, young kids and longtime baseball fans wishing Henry the best, wishing he would break the record and that they would be able to see it when the magic moment happened. For most of the people who wrote him letters, he was their hero.

Then there were the terrible letters, the ones in which anonymous people threatened to kill him and members of his family, the letters that reminded him, in ways even his talent could not deflect, that life was different and often worse for African Americans. One letter was so serious that the FBI removed Henry's daughter from college for her protection. Henry then hired Calvin Wardlaw, a former police officer, as his personal bodyguard. The themes of the letters were all the same: they didn't want him to break the home run record because he was African American. The home run record, the letters said, should not belong to a black person.

"All I did was play baseball to the best of my ability," Henry would say. "And there were so many things I had to deal with, all because of the color of my skin."

When he was having his worst days, he went to visit his family in Mobile, but he wouldn't tell anyone where he was going. He and his brother would go fishing, just to get away from all of the attention, all of the talk that he was unworthy of breaking Ruth's record, and from the death threats that followed him.

One day, sitting in the kitchen with his mother, he asked why he received so much hatred from people he didn't even know.

"Why don't they want me to have something for me, Mama?"

After that conversation, Estella Aaron was convinced more than ever that her son would break the record.

"He told me he was going to do it," Estella said.

"He said, 'I don't want them to forget Babe Ruth. I just want them to remember me.'"

By the time Henry was forty, in 1974, the United States had changed. The Ku Klux Klan still existed, but great people like Jackie Robinson, John F. Kennedy, Rosa Parks, Martin Luther King Jr., John Lewis, and countless others had a dream of their own to make America a place where every person, no matter the color of their skin, could at least have an opportunity to succeed if they were talented and hungry and driven enough. The all-time home run record was something Henry wanted, both for himself and as proof that, given the chance, African Americans could do great things, just like everyone else.

On the last day of the 1973 season, Henry hit home run number 713. He was one home run away from tying the record, but now the season was over and he had to wait the entire winter for a chance to tie Ruth. It was the longest winter of his life. Henry worried and worried about being so close to the record without breaking it. Sometimes, his mind would wander to scary places. He would wonder if the letters were true and not just threats from bad people meant to intimidate him. What if someone shot him before the season started? What if some awful accident happened? He remembered his friend and rival Roberto Clemente, who reached his three-thousandth hit on the last day of the 1972 season and was tragically killed in a plane crash on New Year's Eve. What if Clemente hadn't gotten that last hit in 1972? It would have never come.

Opening day of the 1974 season finally arrived and Henry didn't waste any time. On his very first swing of the season, against the Cincinnati Reds, Henry tied Babe Ruth's record with home run number 714, a no-doubt-about-it shot over the left field fence. The game was stopped and the vice president of the United States walked onto the field to shake Aaron's hand.

Given a microphone to address the cheering crowd, Henry Aaron thanked everyone for their support and then said what was on his mind. "I'm just glad it's almost over with."

On April 8, 1974, at home in Atlanta, Henry started his afternoon sitting on the couch watching soap operas, waiting for when it was time to go to Atlanta–Fulton County Stadium for a game against the Dodgers. Right before game time, Henry looked at his teammate Ralph Garr and said, "Ralph, tonight's the night. I'm going to do it."

The fans booed when Al Downing, the Los Angeles pitcher, walked Henry on four pitches in the first inning. But then in the fourth inning, Downing threw him a hanging breaking ball and Henry lashed it over the left field fence for home run number 715. The crowd went crazy. Henry rounded first, then second, and suddenly, two fans ran onto the field and were running side by side with him. His bodyguard, Calvin, fearing that the fans might have been two of the people who had threatened Henry, reached for his pistol—before seeing the two kids patting Henry on the back.

When he reached home plate, his father stood next to him while his mother was there squeezing her son in joy. When Henry was born, African Americans weren't allowed to play in the major leagues. Now, three months after his fortieth birthday, the kid who once hit bottle caps and dreamed of one day playing baseball held the most celebrated record in American sports.

What did Henry remember the most about that magical night?

"I never knew," Henry said, "that my mother could hug so tight."

Hank Aaron

TOP TEN LIST

Henry Aaron didn't hit the longest home runs. He didn't even really think of himself as a home run hitter at all, but when he retired in 1976, he had hit more than anyone ever. Time and the use of performance-enhancing drugs by many players has changed the all-time home run list and how fans feel about it, but Henry's 755 and Babe Ruth's 714 are still time-treasured numbers for all baseball fans. Here is that all-time home run list.

1. Barry Bonds, PIT-SF, 762
2. Henry Aaron, MIL (NL), ATL, MIL (AL), 755
3. Babe Ruth, BOS (AL), NYY, BOS (NL), 714
4. Willie Mays, NY-SF (NL), NYM (NL), 660
5. Alex Rodriguez, SEA-TEX-NYY, 654
6. Ken Griffey Jr., SEA-CIN-CHW, 630
7. Jim Thome, CLE-PHI-CHW-MIN, 612
8. Sammy Sosa, CHW-TEX-CHC-BAL, 609
9. Frank Robinson, CIN-BAL-CLE-LAA, 586
10. Mark McGwire, OAK-STL, 583

Rickey Henderson

ONE OF A KIND

From the time of the dead-ball era of the 1880s through 1920, as well as in the Negro Leagues, when African Americans were forced to play separately from white players, the roots of baseball had been about getting on base, about forcing the action.

No one forced the action like Rickey Henderson. When he began his rookie year with the Oakland A's in 1979, Rickey was unlike anything the fans had ever seen. Rickey could run and run *fast*. He grew up in Oakland and not only was he a baseball star at Oakland Technical High School but also a football star—and he was built like one, too, like a running back.

But Rickey chose baseball. He became a star for the hometown baseball team, the A's. "I could have played in the NFL. I think I would have been a very good running back," he said. "But I remember it. My mother thought I was too small. She thought I would get hurt. So I played baseball to keep her from worrying."

There have always been players who were fast. Harry Hooper, who played for the Boston Red Sox in the early 1900s, was fast. So were Ty Cobb and Jackie Robinson. So was Maury Wills, who, in 1962, stole over 100 bases in a season for the Dodgers, and the Montreal Expos' Tim Raines, who stole at least 70 bases six seasons in a row back in the 80s. Today there is Billy Hamilton with the Cincinnati Reds, a young player with a lot of stolen bases in his future.

There were also players who were both fast *and* strong. Guys like Henry Aaron and Willie Mays, Mickey Mantle and Joe DiMaggio, Barry Bonds and Mike Trout. There were even a couple of guys who were fast and strong and hit first in the order. Before having a son named Barry, who would become even more famous than his all-star dad, Bobby Bonds had been that type of player. Bobby Bonds hit at least 30 home runs while stealing at least 30 bases five times in his career, most of the time from the leadoff spot. Then there was Lou Brock, who played from 1961 to 1980, mostly with the St. Louis Cardinals. Brock could run and hit for power, too. Though he never hit more than 21 home runs in a season, Brock was consistently among the league leaders in stolen bases, doubles, and triples. When he retired, Brock held the all-time records for stolen bases in a season (118) and in a career (938).

Rickey was different from them all. Yes, he was fast and strong and he was a leadoff hitter. Yet baseball had never seen a leadoff hitter like Rickey. Like Bonds, Henderson hit for power. But *unlike* Bonds, Rickey did not strike out much. Bobby Bonds didn't just strike out a lot, he led the league in strikeouts multiple times from the position where it was most crucial to get on base. Bonds struck out an astounding 1,757 times over 14 seasons—an average of 125 per season—and hit just .268 for his career. Despite his speed, Bonds seemed to be a hitter miscast in the leadoff role. Rickey struck out 100 times in his career only once—the year he turned 40!

Brock was clearly the preeminent base-stealer of his generation, the one with all of the records. Brock was the engine of the great Cardinals teams that won championships, as Rickey would be with his winning teams.

The difference was that Rickey was an even better player than Brock, who was a Hall of Famer. To begin with, despite leading the league in stolen bases eight times, Brock was *caught* stealing—or thrown out—25 percent of his attempts, or once every four tries. Rickey, who attempted over *500* more steals than Brock, was caught less than 20 percent of the time. In other words, Rickey took more chances and was significantly more likely to steal a base safely. And unlike Brock (and Bonds), Rickey had a great eye for the strike zone. He wouldn't swing at balls very often unless they were strikes. The reward for his patience at the plate was that he walked often. Walks meant getting on base, and getting on base was the name of the game for a leadoff hitter. Getting on base meant a chance that Rickey would steal or score a run. In his twenty-five years in the Major Leagues, Henderson had a career on-base percentage of .400. For comparison's sake, Brock's career on-base percentage was .343. Rickey led the league in walks four times and in runs scored five times. He also hit close to 300 home runs, more than twice Brock's figure.

Henderson, in short, would become the greatest leadoff hitter of all time. He would steal more bases than anyone to ever play the game. He would score more runs than anyone to ever play the game. He would walk more times than anyone to ever play the game. And he would hit more leadoff home runs than anyone to ever play the game. Not all of those records would last (most records don't), but some still stand today.

Like Mays and Aaron before him, Henderson was a five-tool player: he hit for average, hit for power, ran the bases with speed, played strong defense in the outfield, and had a strong enough arm to throw runners out. He had the speed of a center fielder combined with the power of a third baseman. In his first full season in the majors, he led the league in steals with 100, a level he would reach three times. Starting with that first full year, he would go on to lead the league in steals seven straight seasons. In his fourth season he broke Brock's single-season stolen base record of 118 by swiping a whopping 130.

The numbers, though, tell only a small portion of who Rickey Henderson was or what he meant to the game of baseball. He was the last of a generation of great base-stealers. He was one of the first, however, to spend his entire career in the new world of free agency, where players could change teams when their contracts expired. Rickey would become the most traveled Hall of Famer ever.

Henderson was dynamic and beloved in Oakland, the kind of player the fans came to the ballpark to see. However, as his contract came close to renewal, the A's decided they did not want to pay Henderson the kind of salary they knew he would demand. In 1985, they traded Rickey to the Yankees, a team loaded with offensive power. Yankees outfielder Dave Winfield, who would be elected to the Hall of Fame, was on that team, as was Don Mattingly, the power-hitting, run-producing first baseman. Don Baylor, the slugging designated hitter and one-time league MVP, was there, too. Not surprisingly, the Yankees scored a lot of runs and won a lot of games.

Yet they did not pitch well enough to ever make the playoffs, and the fans—as well as Yankees owner George Steinbrenner—blamed Henderson and Winfield. They blamed Henderson for making a lot of money and for not playing in as many games as they thought he should. Henderson had always missed games because of his rugged style of play. Stealing bases, diving back to first, diving headfirst into second all put a lot of strain on Rickey's body.

Henderson had posted great offensive numbers in New York, but he was not beloved by the fans or the team in New York. He was known for voicing his opinions about money. If he felt another player shouldn't be making more than he was, he would say it, which made him unpopular with the players *and* the fans.

Midway through the 1989 season, Henderson was traded back to the Oakland A's, who by that time were on their way to becoming one of the most talented teams of all time. Frustrated, feeling as though he was unfairly blamed for the Yankees not making the playoffs, Rickey took off, going on a tear that pushed the A's, who had reached the World Series the previous year (only to lose to the Dodgers), into the playoffs.

With Rickey, the A's were unstoppable. Rickey played 85 games with the 1989 A's and had 90 hits. When the A's went back to the postseason, Henderson almost singlehandedly destroyed Toronto in the American League Championship Series, hitting .400 with eight stolen bases and two home runs in a five-game wipeout. He was named MVP of the series.

In the World Series against San Francisco, Rickey hit .474 with a home run and three stolen bases in a four-game sweep.

The next year, Rickey continued the blistering performance he'd delivered in the playoffs. Over the full 1990 season, he won the American League MVP, hitting .325 with 28 home runs, 119 runs scored, and 65 stolen bases, leading the A's back to the World Series. This time, though, the A's were swept in four straight by the Reds.

The A's made the playoffs again in 1992, but lost to Toronto in the ALCS. The next year, the guy who had earned the nickname "Man of Steal" was traded to Toronto and ended up standing on second base for one of the most famous moments in baseball history, when Joe Carter hit a World Series–winning home run to beat Philadelphia. Rickey was a champion again.

At the end of 1998, when he led the league in stolen bases again at age thirty-nine, Henderson was asked by reporters if he planned on retiring. He said "No, not now. Maybe when I'm fifty." He sounded like Satchel Paige, the great Negro League pitcher who once said, "Maybe I'll pitch forever," and in 1965, at age fifty-nine, actually appeared in a Major League game for the Kansas City A's!

So, on Rickey went, to the Mets for a couple of years, and then the Mariners, Padres, Angels, and even the Red Sox and Dodgers, who signed him at the ages of forty-three and forty-four. Finally, after thirty games in the 2003 season, the Dodgers released Henderson. He was forty-four years old and never officially retired from baseball. He always expected the phone to ring, for another team who needed help to give him a call.

It never did.

Rickey Henderson played for nine different teams, for San Diego twice and for Oakland on three different occasions. He played for both New York teams and both Los Angeles teams. Had he played for the Texas Rangers during the latter part of his career, he would have played for every team in the American League West! He played in the World Series three times and won it twice.

Over Rickey's twenty-five years in the game, baseball began to realize how valuable and rare a talent he was. He ended up playing in four different decades. He amassed 3,055 hits. He was one of the game's great personalities. And of course, he was the perfect leadoff hitter. In 2008, the perfect leadoff hitter wound up in the perfect place: the Hall of Fame.

TOP TEN LIST

Rickey Henderson was the greatest leadoff hitter of all time. He was also the greatest base-stealer of all time. He led the league in steals eleven times, including seven years in a row from 1980–1986. Here are the all-time leaders in stolen bases:

1. Rickey Henderson—1,406
2. Lou Brock—938
3. Billy Hamilton (not the Billy Hamilton you may know from today's game; this Billy Hamilton played from 1881 to 1901)—914
4. Ty Cobb—897
5. Tim Raines—808
6. Vince Coleman—752
7. Arlie Latham—742
8. Eddie Collins—741
9. Max Carey—738
10. Honus Wagner—723

Summer

Miracle!

THE 1914 BOSTON BRAVES

L inus van Pelt: "Winning isn't everything, Charlie Brown . . ."
Charlie Brown: "That's true, but losing isn't *anything*!"

Six years after the Civil War ended, in 1871, Boston received its first professional baseball team. No, it wasn't the Red Sox, which would come later, in 1901, but the Boston Red Stockings, a long-lost team nobody's ever heard of.

Or have they?

The Red Stockings still exist today, but you

might not realize it because they play in Atlanta as the Atlanta Braves. Between their inception in 1871 and 1914, the Red Stockings were known for two things: name changes and, after a successful beginning, losing badly. In 1883, they were known as the Beaneaters, a name they carried until 1907, when Bostonians began referring to them as the Doves and after that, the Rustlers, until one name, the Braves, finally stuck through the years in Boston and later when the franchise moved to Milwaukee in 1953 and then to Atlanta in 1966.

Name changes were not uncommon back then. Team nicknames were just that, and they changed often. The Red Sox were originally known as the Boston Pilgrims and the Boston Americans; the Yankees were the New York Highlanders.

What was uncommon was the way the Red Stockings-Beaneaters-Doves-Rustlers-Braves would lose games. Things started off well enough. In two of their first three years of existence, the Red Stockings finished in first place. In 1892, the Beaneaters won 102 games and beat the Cleveland Spiders in the Championship Series. They were first again in 1893 and again in 1897 and 1898.

Then came 1900, when they finished in fourth place, beginning a string of 14 straight seasons of "these-guys-are-the-worst-epic-fail" awfulness. The team finished in last place four straight years from 1909 to 1912 and in the 11 seasons from 1903 to 1913 never posted a winning record and never finished higher than fifth place.

The 1914 season figured to be much of the same. They started the season losing their first three games to the Brooklyn Dodgers and Philadelphia Phillies, lost 10 of their first 13 games, and before the spring weather arrived were already 10 games out of first place.

Another long summer of losing was on its way.

The Braves were afterthoughts, even in their own city. Two years earlier, in 1912, the Red Sox had built their brand-new ballpark, Fenway Park, while the Braves toiled at the old, run-down South End Grounds. One city, two very different teams.

In their first year at new Fenway Park, the Red Sox won the World Series. In 1914, while the Braves couldn't win a game, the Red Sox had an upstart rookie pitcher named Babe Ruth, who seemed to have big plans for himself—and the ability to back it up.

The Braves had two veteran players, Johnny Evers and Rabbit Maranville, who were once stars and would one day be inducted into the Baseball Hall of Fame, but it was hard to notice them when the team was in last place.

On Monday, June 8, the Boston Braves lost 3–2 to Cincinnati, leaving them in last place with a record of 12–28, thirteen games behind the powerful New York Giants. A month later, on July 4, they lost both ends of a doubleheader to Brooklyn, had lost five games in a row, and were now fifteen games behind the Giants.

Season over. Wait till next year. Right?

Then, something began happening.

Two days later, on July 6, the Braves played another doubleheader against the Dodgers and won both games. And then they won again. And again and again. They won six in a row to get out of last place, and then won nine more in a row to finally reach the .500 mark.

Something else happened. The Braves abandoned their beat-up home field in August and struck a deal with the Red Sox, agreeing to play the remainder of their games at Fenway Park when the Red Sox were out of town.

On August 13, the Braves had climbed all the way to second place when they traveled to New York, to the famed Polo Grounds for a showdown with the first-place Giants. The Braves had shaved 10 games off the Giants' lead. Boston then beat the New Yorkers three straight.

The Giants' lead was now only 3 1/2 games. Could the team that never seemed to win actually take first place?

That's exactly what happened on August 25, when the Braves tied the Giants for first place with a 7–1 win in Philadelphia. A new nickname had begun to take hold by this point: the "Miracle Braves." And that miracle, it turns out, was just getting started.

By the end of the season, the Boston Braves had steamrolled everyone, beating the New York Giants and the Brooklyn Dodgers to end the season and winning the National League pennant by an amazing 10 1/2 games! They had gone 68–19 after July 4. No team in baseball history had come from so far behind to win the pennant by so many games—and none have, even to this day.

The pennant was one thing, but the World Series was another, as the Braves would play one of the great teams of all time: the Philadelphia Athletics (yes, the same Athletics that now call Oakland home). The A's were stacked with great players across the diamond, from the pitchers Chief Bender and Eddie Plank to third baseman Frank "Home Run" Baker. The A's had already won the World Series in 1911 and were the defending World Series champs, having beaten the Giants in 1913 to become winners once again. This was the team of manager Connie Mack's famed "$100,000 infield" of Stuffy McInnis at first, Eddie Collins at second, Jack Barry at short, and Baker at third. This was an A's team that seemingly couldn't lose.

The truth was, they couldn't win. The Miracle Braves, still the hottest team in baseball, destroyed the A's in four straight games, winning the World Series.

The nickname was an appropriate one. Nobody could explain it. The Miracle Braves had been losers from 1903 to that strange summer of 1914, when they suddenly beat everyone and won the World Series. The next year, the Braves finished second, then third in 1916. Just as suddenly, they went back to losing. By 1917, they were the same old Braves, finishing 25 games out of first. They didn't have a winning record again for another 15 years, failed to make the World Series again until 1948, and didn't manage to win another World Series until 1957, four years after leaving Boston and moving to Milwaukee.

Over the years, there would be other miracles; In 1967, the Boston Red Sox reached the World Series after having not enjoyed a winning season since 1957. In 1969, the New York Mets went from having never had a winning season to winning the World Series. The Boston Braves, however, were the first. It didn't make sense then, and it doesn't make sense now, but for one summer, they were the best team in the world.

TOP TEN LIST

The 1914 Braves staged one of the greatest comebacks in the history of baseball, but they weren't alone. Over the past one hundred years, more than a few teams have made spectacular comebacks that history will never forget. Remember, the season's not over until it's over.

1. 1964 Cardinals: Trailed Philadelphia by 6 1/2 games with 12 to play. Won NL pennant and World Series.
2. 2007 Rockies: 4 1/2 games back with only nine left to play. Reached World Series.
3. 1993 Braves: 10 games behind San Francisco Giants on July 22. Won NL West Division on last day of season.
4. 1978 Yankees: 14 games behind Red Sox on July

20. Beat Red Sox in one-game playoff to win division and went on to win the World Series.

5. 1969 Mets: 9 1/2 games behind Cubs on August 13. Won World Series.

6. 1951 Giants: Trailed Dodgers by 13 1/2 games on August 11. Reached World Series.

7. 1995 Mariners: Trailed Angels by 13 1/2 games. Beat Angels in one-game playoff to win division.

8. 2011 Rays: Trailed Red Sox by 9 games on September 4. Reached playoffs as the wild card team with a win on the final day of season that put them ahead of Boston.

9. 1949 Yankees: Trailed Red Sox by one game with two to play. Won both games, the pennant, and later the World Series.

10. 2011 Cardinals: Trailed Atlanta for the wild card by 8 1/2 games on September 6. Ended up winning World Series.

The Boys of Summer

THE 1947–55 BROOKLYN DODGERS

"IF IT WEREN'T FOR THE YANKEES . . ." How many times over the course of baseball history have those very words been uttered? By how many players? By how many teams? Over how many years? The New York Yankees aren't just the greatest winners in the history of American sports, but they're also the greatest party crashers in the history of sport, ruining the dreams of so many other good teams that would have been remembered as great if only they could have beaten the Yankees.

Imagine ending up in the World Series *five* times over the course of twelve years. You would take that offer, right? Yet that is exactly what the Brooklyn Dodgers—and their fans—experienced, heading to the World Series in 1941, 1947, 1949, 1952, and 1953 . . . only to lose to the same team each time: the Yankees.

There are so many teams that history has erased, unfairly perhaps, because they couldn't win the big games, or because when they did, they couldn't beat the Yankees. The Boston Red Sox of the 1970s were a terrific team, who played in arguably the single greatest World Series ever in 1975 (more on that later in the book), but they played little brother to the Yankees' big brother for the rest of the decade.

The difference between the Brooklyn Dodgers and every other team frustrated by the mighty Yankees was that the Dodgers actually left town! It was bad enough that the Yankees so thoroughly dominated their crosstown rivals—now Dodgers fans had to watch their hometown heroes move all the way across the country. Talk about adding insult to injury . . .

Yet history shows us that these Dodgers weren't

just an afterthought compared to the Yankees. These were the Dodgers of Jackie Robinson, the team that changed history because it was the first to have a black player, and in those days many Americans were not sure that African Americans and whites could play together, could be friends, or could even trust each other. This fear was held whether the subject was baseball or being in the army or simply being neighbors. Robinson signaled the start of a new, modern America, the roots of how things are today—and it started on the baseball field.

Maybe the players, or at least some of them, knew how important they were. Robinson certainly did, and maybe it was part of the reason for their success. Or maybe the Dodgers were just good, because for nearly a decade the Dodgers destroyed the rest of the National League. Either way, this team touched people who would go on to honor them in turn, in public statements and in books—a quality far more lasting and important than winning and losing. People who lived in Brooklyn or were Dodgers fans at that time surely remember that the Yankees almost always won, but they remember, too, how the Dodgers made them *feel*. This was the team made famous years later by one book, Roger Kahn's classic *The Boys of Summer*.

After a slow start in 1947, Robinson took off and the Dodgers soared. Robinson was the hungriest of players, who did not do any one thing great, but did everything well. He could hit for a high average. He could hit a home run. He could steal bases—which he did daringly—and he could field, and he played with a sense of competition that even his greatest adversaries, both on and off the field, could admire.

The 1947 Dodgers won the pennant over St. Louis by five games. It was a complete team. Pee Wee Reese was the captain and a perennial all-star at shortstop. When the fans in Cincinnati began hurling racial insults at Robinson one day, Reese, who was white, went over and put his arm around Jackie's shoulder as a symbol of unity. Reese was so respected that the crowd grew silent. He and Robinson led the team in home runs with just 12, but the Dodgers were terrific—until the World Series, where they lost to the Yankees in seven heartbreaking games.

The 1949 team saw Robinson win the league Most Valuable Player Award, and it won the pennant by a single game over St. Louis, only to lose the World Series in five games. To the Yankees, of course.

It was in the 1950s, however, that the Boys of Summer really took off. In addition to Reese and Robinson, Duke Snider was the power-hitting center fielder who joined the Yankees' Mickey Mantle and the Giants' Willie Mays in the trio of great center fielders all playing in New York at the same time. Gil Hodges was the beloved and rugged first baseman who could hit home runs and play defense with the best of them. The Dodgers had all-star players at virtually every position, including Roy Campanella, who would become one of the greatest catchers of all time, and like Robinson, one of the first great black players in Major League history.

Even the players who were not famous were still very good. Billy Cox was the best defensive third baseman in the game, and in right field, Carl Furillo boasted a powerful arm. The 1952 team, which lost to the Yankees in seven games, also featured Joe Black, who became the first African American pitcher to win a World Series game.

The 1953 team was one of the very best in history.

The Dodgers won 105 games, averaged more than 6 runs per game, won the pennant by 13 games over a rising Milwaukee Braves team, and won 60 of 77 games at Ebbets Field. This was the year the Yankees would finally feel what it felt like to lose, right?

Wrong. The Yankees won the first two games of that season's World Series at Yankee Stadium, lost the next two in Brooklyn, then won a pivotal Game 5, 11–7, in Brooklyn.

The next day, Game 6 in Yankee Stadium, the Yankees were up 3–1 with one out in the ninth, two outs away from a fifth straight championship, when Duke Snider walked. Allie Reynolds, the Yankee pitcher, then gave up a game-tying two-run homer. The Dodgers' magical season appeared to be saved— that is, until the bottom of the ninth, when Billy Martin hit a one-out single up the middle to win the game. And the championship.

The Dodgers, heartbroken, had lost again.

Whether it isn't being as tall or as fast as you'd like to be or whether a ground ball rolls up the middle *just far enough away* to be a hit instead of an out, life isn't fair, they say. Life certainly doesn't always make sense, which might explain why the 1955 Dodgers, probably the weakest of all those powerhouse Dodgers teams, happened to be the team that finally beat the Yankees. Jackie Robinson was thirty-six, still fiery, but weakened as a player. Cox was gone, and Robinson played third base. Furillo was thirty-three, Reese thirty-six. This was an aging team at the tail end of its great run.

Still, the Dodgers won 98 games, and crushed the ball as usual. Campanella, Hodges, and Snider all drove in more than 100 runs. Don Newcombe won 20 games, but no one else won more than 11. They won the National League pennant by 13 1/2 games and won 56 games at Ebbets Field. Of course, it was the Yankees who awaited them in the World Series, for the sixth time.

The Yankees won the first two games at Yankee Stadium, then the Dodgers came home and evened the series at 2–2, with Campanella homering in Game 3. Campanella, Hodges, and Snider each hit homers in the Game 4 win.

Duke Snider was on fire, hitting two more home runs in Game 5 and propelling the Dodgers to a 3-games-to-2 lead in the series. The Dodgers headed back to Yankee Stadium needing just one win over the final two games to become champions. In Game 6, the Yankees scored five runs in the very first inning and rolled to a win behind the pitching of Whitey Ford. The World Series would come down to a winner-takes-all seventh game.

Tuesday, October 4, 1955, in front of 62,465 fans, 23-year-old Johnny Podres, who grew up in Witherbee, New York, pitched the game of his life. With the Dodgers up 2–0 in the bottom of the eighth, two on and one out, Podres was in trouble. Yet he coaxed Yogi Berra to fly out to right and then struck out Hank Bauer. Inning over, Dodgers still in front.

In the ninth, the Yankees, the vaunted Bronx Bombers, went quietly, and when Elston Howard grounded out to Reese at short, it was over. The Dodgers, the *Brooklyn Dodgers,* founded in 1884, who had lost the World Series in 1916, 1941, 1947, 1949, 1952, and 1953, were finally champions! Podres would spend the rest of his life a hero to Dodgers fans.

The 1956 season would feel familiar to fans of the Brooklyn Dodgers. The team played valiant baseball once again during the season, catching and and eventually taking down Milwaukee to win the pennant. It was back to the World Series and back to facing the Yankees. It would be another seven-game thriller, but this time the Yankees were back to their winning ways.

Over the following winter the Dodgers did the unthinkable and traded Robinson, their fiercest competitor, to the New York Giants. Yet Robinson had already decided to retire, so he never played a single game for the Giants. Reese's best seasons were also behind him and he would retire two years later.

1957 really did spell the end for the Brooklyn Dodgers. Secretly, both the Dodgers and Giants had made a deal to leave town forever, to be the first big-league teams to play in California. After the 1957 season, the Dodgers made their move to Los Angeles, the Giants to San Francisco. The National League would not field a baseball team in New York for four full seasons until the New York Mets were founded in 1962.

On the field there can be only one winner. The Dodgers were great, but the Yankees were and would always be the greatest winners in the history of the game. Baseball and sports in general, however, are about so much more than winning, and the Brooklyn Dodgers, even though they would be no more, even though they would move to Los Angeles, would endure in the national imagination. Perhaps it's because they left. Perhaps it's because America loves a good underdog story, and when faced with the dominance of the mighty Yankees, the Brooklyn Dodgers were a team everyone else could root for. Perhaps it's because of what they represented as people and what they meant to their time. The late 1940s and 1950s were an extremely important time in America, when World War II had ended and courageous people demanded that everyone be treated more fairly at home. It was on the baseball field, of all places, where changes in American society could first be seen, and that, far more than winning or losing to the Yankees, is why the Brooklyn Dodgers of Jackie and Pee Wee, and Duke and Campy, are still important to this very day.

The 1947–55 Brooklyn Dodgers

TOP TEN LIST

The Brooklyn Dodgers are no more, having moved from Brooklyn to Los Angeles after the 1957 season. It was a shock then and it's history now, but many of today's teams started out somewhere else. Some of the nicknames may be the same, but the cities have changed. Here are ten moves worth following.

1. Athletics (Philadelphia 1901–1954. Kansas City 1955–1967. Oakland 1968–present)
2. Braves (Boston 1883–1952. Milwaukee 1953–1965. Atlanta 1966–present)
3. Orioles (St. Louis Browns 1901–1953. Baltimore Orioles 1954–present)
4. Twins (Washington Senators 1901–1960. Minnesota Twins 1961–present)
5. Rangers (Washington Senators 1961–1971. Texas Rangers 1972–present)

6. Nationals (Montreal Expos 1969–2004.
   Washington Nationals 2005–present)

7. Giants (New York Giants 1883–1957. San Francisco
   Giants 1958–present)

8. Yankees (Baltimore Orioles 1901–1902. New York
   Highlanders 1903–1912. New York Yankees 1913–
   present)

9. Brewers (Seattle Pilots 1969. Milwaukee Brewers
   (AL) 1970–1996. Milwaukee Brewers (NL) 1997–
   present)

10. Angels (Los Angeles Angels 1961. Also played
    as the Anaheim Angels, California Angels, and
    presently, the Los Angeles Angels of Anaheim)

The Outlaws

~~~~~~

THE 1972–74 OAKLAND A's

The 1960s were one of the most tumultuous decades in American history. So many areas of society changed. Thanks to the civil rights movement, people of all colors were finally, after nearly two hundred years, protected under the law. America endured a long, bitter war in Vietnam that changed the way citizens viewed their government and the place of war in society. A growing movement to guarantee the rights of women would soon give women opportunities in America that did not exist before. In many ways, change was taking place in America so fast, people had difficulty keeping up.

Baseball was no different. Players and owners had never really gotten along, mostly because the players were underpaid and worse, for more than a hundred years, they were not allowed to change teams when their contracts expired. It wasn't until the 1960s that the players began to organize as a group and fight the owners for their rights. If a guy who worked at a coffee shop or as a teacher or a lawyer was allowed to change whom he worked for, why couldn't a baseball player?

The changes in the culture from the 1960s created a different kind of baseball player as the 1970s began. The 1970s players wore their hair longer, wore sideburns and mustaches. They spoke out more. In 1972, the players even went on strike for nine days, refusing to play until the owners improved their pension benefits.

The best team of the early 1970s, the Oakland A's, also best represented this change. This was a different type of team for a different type of game. Baseball had always been considered one of the most traditional institutions in America, but the A's weren't interested in following tradition. For one hundred years, baseball players wore black baseball spikes. The A's wore white baseball shoes. Players were often expected to be clean-cut and clean-shaven, as if they were in the military. The A's wore mustaches and beards and long hair. Most baseball teams had two uniforms: home and away. The A's owned five different uniform combinations. Some were all green. Some were all yellow. Some were green-and-yellow. Some were white.

The purists, the ones who felt baseball should never change, were outraged that the A's dressed like a softball team and looked like a motorcycle gang. They were outraged at the owner of the team, Charlie Finley, who, in their eyes, showed no respect for baseball traditions, making his team look like circus clowns.

And the players, well, the Oakland A's were a group of big personalities who did not always (or sometimes at all) like each other, but for three straight years, when they stepped on the field there was no better team. From 1972 until 1974 they won three straight World Series championships.

Everything that seemed new and different about the A's wasn't. When the A's won their first World

Series in 1972, beating Cincinnati in seven games, the club had only been in Oakland for five years, but the Athletics name was one of the oldest in baseball. They were first the Philadelphia Athletics, the team that dominated baseball from 1910 to 1914 and again from 1929 to 1932. In both cases, the owner, Connie Mack, found himself short on money despite having great teams, and he wound up breaking up his winning teams by selling off all of the A's superstar players to other teams. The A's fell on hard times and in 1955 they moved to Kansas City, where Finley bought them in 1960. The team played in Kansas City from 1955 to 1967 and never enjoyed a winning season.

In Oakland, the A's had amassed an impressive group of players, just rising to power. The A's finished 82–80 in their first year in Oakland.

There was Jim "Catfish" Hunter, a right-hander from North Carolina who did not fish and did not particularly like catfish, either. Instead, Finley had chosen the nickname to give him "personality."

There was right-handed pitcher John "Blue Moon" Odom, who received his nickname as a child because his head was supposedly as round as the moon. And there was left-handed pitcher Vida Blue, a rookie sensation. Rollie Fingers, whose handlebar mustache made him look like a saloonkeeper from the 1800s, was the best relief pitcher in the game. The shortstop went by the name Campy Campaneris (his first name was actually Bert). There was Reggie Jackson, the young, brash, left-handed power hitter from Wyncote, Pennsylvania, who would become an all-time great.

Each of them did things as colorful as their nicknames. Jackson was the biggest star, a slugger who swung like Babe Ruth. One time, at the 1971 All-Star Game in Detroit, he hit a home run off Pittsburgh's Dock Ellis that appeared headed to the moon if the floodlights high above Tiger Stadium hadn't gotten in the way. In a game full of all stars, Reggie found a way to steal the show. Even when he struck out, which was often, he would leave fans in awe because of how hard he swung.

Each of these strong personalities had their reasons for disliking one another. Blue and Odom once got into a fistfight during the 1972 playoffs, as did Fingers and Blue, but the A's did have one thing that united them as a team: their dislike of Finley, the owner who, they felt, underpaid them. The players believed he cheated them out of money he had promised them.

They were the strangest bunch, playing in green and gold uniforms and white shoes, fighting with themselves and with their owner. Once, when the team arrived in Detroit, a woman seeking an autograph approached Reggie Jackson. "Mr. Jackson, are there any more of your friends on that bus?" Jackson looked at the woman and said, "Ain't no friends on that bus."

Finley tried every promotional trick to encourage fans to come see his team and to change the traditions of baseball. He changed the team's mascot—historically an elephant since 1904—to a mule. Once, he petitioned the commissioner's office to use fluorescent orange baseballs instead of white, to make them easier for players to see (that one never caught on).

When it came time to concentrate on the field and play championship baseball, however, few teams in history did it like this one.

In their first trip to the playoffs in 1971, the A's were swept in three straight games by the defending

World Series champion Baltimore Orioles. However, the next year, the A's took off. The A's faced Detroit and won a tight five-game series. Odom and Blue combined on a five-hitter to win a deciding fifth game and send the A's to their first World Series since 1931, when the team was based in Philadelphia.

In the series, the A's faced another budding powerhouse, the Cincinnati Reds, soon to be known as the Big Red Machine. The A's were without Reggie Jackson, who had injured himself against Detroit. Blue saved the first game; Catfish Hunter won the second. Home in Cincinnati for Game 3, the Reds' Jack Billingham outdueled Odom, 1–0, but the A's rallied in Game 4 with two runs in the bottom of the ninth to win 3–2 and bring them within a game for the first Major League Championship in the San Francisco Bay Area.

The A's, however, lost the next two games, forcing a winner-takes-all showdown. In Game 7, Odom was handed the ball to start, but it was Hunter, who entered the game in relief, who wound up the winning pitcher, 3–2. Fingers closed out the game for the save. The A's were champions. Little-known catcher Gene

Tenace hit .348 and was named the series MVP.

The next year, featuring a pitching staff that had three 20-game winners, the A's would dominate the American League's regular season. In the playoffs they found sweet revenge for their loss in '71 by beating Baltimore in the American League Championship Series, reaching the World Series for a second consecutive year, this time facing the surprise New York Mets. The Mets featured the best pitcher in the game, the great Tom Seaver, and 42-year-old Willie Mays, a fading Hall of Fame talent making the final appearances of his legendary 22-year career.

The teams split the first six games, forcing a deciding seventh game for the second straight year. In the finale, Jackson, back and recharged, hit his first World Series home run on his way to being named series MVP.

After a long drought, the A's had won back-to-back World Series.

The A's continued their roll through the 1974 season, beat Baltimore again in the playoffs, and faced the Los Angeles Dodgers in the first all-California World Series.

This one ended quickly. The A's were too good, too sharp, and too talented. They beat the Dodgers in five games. Hunter got a win and a save. Jackson homered, but this time it was Fingers, who appeared in four of the five games and saved two, who won the MVP.

The A's were champions again, becoming the first and only team in baseball other than the Yankees to ever win three straight World Series titles.

History has a way of repeating itself. True to the team's historical roots, Finley was out of money and sold off this Oakland A's championship team the same way Mack had sold off the 1910–1914 and the 1929–1931 Philadelphia A's teams. Oakland had its run of championships interrupted not by opponents on the field, but by big business off of it. Catfish Hunter, owed money by Finley, successfully sued him for breach of contract, became a free agent, and signed a $3 million deal with the Yankees. Jackson would be traded to Baltimore, before signing with the Yankees as a free agent. Outfielder Joe Rudi would later join the Red Sox and then the California Angels, while Vida Blue would join the San Francisco Giants. Rollie Fingers became a San Diego Padre.

Finley's antics would rob a great team of something they had truly deserved—the right to be considered one of the all-time greatest teams—but it was only temporary, because Fingers, Jackson, Hunter, and Dick Williams, the manager of the title teams in 1972 and 1973, all ended up in the Hall of Fame. They were that good.

And so were the A's.

The 1972–74 Oakland A's

TOP TEN LIST

The green-and-yellow uniforms, white shoes, and distinctive personalities made the A's a colorful team, but nothing made them more memorable (outside of winning three World Series titles in a row) than their nicknames. More than any other sport, baseball has the best nicknames. Catfish and Blue Moon have lots of company. Here are ten (okay, eleven; this one was just too hard to narrow down!) awesome nicknames.

1. Oil Can Boyd (Dennis Boyd, 1982–1991)
2. Chicken Wolf (William Van Winkle Wolf, 1882–1892)
3. The Only Nolan (Edward Sylvester Nolan, 1878–1885)
4. Moonlight Graham (Archibald Graham, 1905)
5. Teddy Ballgame (Ted Williams, 1939–1960)

6. The Yankee Clipper (Joe DiMaggio, 1936–1951)

7. The Say Hey Kid (Willie Mays, 1951–1973)

8. Pee Wee Reese (Harold Reese, 1940–1958)

9. Shoeless Joe Jackson (Joe Jackson, 1908–1920)

10. Scrap Iron Garner (Phil Garner, 1973–1988)

11. The Mad Hungarian (Al Hrabowsky, 1970–1982)

Saved

THE 1993 SAN FRANCISCO GIANTS

hen you're a kid, few things are more important than your favorite team. It is a member of the family, as close and meaningful as a pet or a little brother. The summers are marked by playing baseball, watching baseball, and going to games wearing the hat and colors of the home team. You and your team are one and the same.

In 1992, the San Francisco Giants, the team that had been in the same city since Major League Baseball first moved out west in 1957, announced it would be moving to Saint Petersburg, Florida. Big business and money were trying to get in the way of the fun, and fans everywhere in San Francisco were getting ready to see their team leave town. The team wanted a new stadium to replace cold and windy Candlestick Park, but the city wouldn't build one for them. The Giants took their case directly to the public, hoping voters in San Francisco and the San Jose area would force the politicians to build them a new stadium. But the voters said no, too.

So the Giants looked and looked around the country for a place that *would* build them a new stadium, and Saint Petersburg was just the place. It wasn't even a promise of what might be: The stadium was already built. All the Giants had to do was pack up and leave.

It looked like history repeating itself, really, because in 1957, kids all over Harlem and the rest of New York City had felt the pain of the New York Giants—their team since 1883—leaving town for California for the promise of a new stadium. Nearly forty years later, the kids in San Francisco were feeling the same way when the team announced it was planning to move to Florida for the same reason.

The difference was, Superman must have been on vacation when the Giants were still in New York because there were no heroes to save the New York Giants. They left for California. The San Francisco Giants, however, got lucky. A group of local businessmen bought the Giants from their previous owner, Robert Lurie, and promised to keep the team in San Francisco. They promised to do something else, too: make the team good again. The Giants had been to the World Series as recently as 1989, only to lose to their crosstown rivals, the Oakland A's. It had been all downhill from there, culminating in a ninety-loss season in 1992. There was no way around it—this team was bad.

In the winter of 1992, the Giants went out and signed the best player in the world, left fielder Barry Bonds, to a massive (at the time), six-year, $43 million contract. Bonds had won two Most Valuable Player Awards with the Pittsburgh Pirates and, along with Ken Griffey Jr. of Seattle, was considered the best all-around player in the game. Bonds was a dream player:

He could run, throw, hit for average, hit for power, and he did it with the kind of style and flair that made people notice. There was an added bonus, too: Barry Bonds was from the San Francisco area. His father, Bobby, had also begun his career for the Giants, and Barry's godfather was none other than the greatest Giant of them all, Willie Mays.

The Giants immediately went about creating a sense of connection between the team and city, to re-mind San Franciscans that the Giants were as big a part of the city as the Golden Gate Bridge. They hired a new manager, Dusty Baker, who had grown up in Sacramento, just a couple of hours to the east, and hired Barry's father, Bobby, to be the first-base coach. They pledged that the legends of the great Giants teams of the past—Mays, Willie McCovey, Juan Marichal—would be around the ballpark to meet fans. After being so close to leaving, the Giants' new owner Peter Magowan showed the hometown fans that the Giants would forever be a part of the San Francisco community.

Once the season started, no one quite knew what to expect. Sure, the fans were excited that the Giants were staying, but they had lost ninety games the year before. Would they be any good? And in 1993, $43 million was the richest contract in baseball history. How could Bonds, as good as he was, live up to that pressure?

He did, and the team embarked on a magical summer. Bonds drove in the winning run in the very first game of the season. On May 11, Bonds hit a double and a triple, third baseman Matt Williams hit a home run, and the Giants beat Colorado to take the lead in their division.

The Atlanta Braves, who at the time were in the same division as the Giants, had been known as the best team in the league, having appeared in the last two World Series, yet all of a sudden the Giants surpassed them. The Giants were the most exciting team in baseball. During much of the first half of the season, Bonds was hitting over .400.

On June 24, the Giants rapped twenty hits and belted five home runs in a 17–2 win over Colorado, boosting their lead in the National League West all the way to nine games. The city of San Francisco, once again, was in love with baseball.

Baseball, however, is a long season. Sensing that

the Giants might just run away with the whole season, Atlanta looked to San Diego, a team that was struggling both on the field and financially. The Padres were hoping to trade all of their best players to save money. They traded power-hitting Gary Sheffield to the Los Angeles Dodgers, and moved Fred McGriff, one of the most dangerous home run hitters in the game, to the Braves.

That trade changed the season. With McGriff, the Braves had the power hitter they had lacked, and they soared with newfound energy.

The fall of the Giants came quickly. On August 23, leading the division by 7 1/2 games, San Francisco hosted Atlanta. Led by future Hall of Fame pitchers Tom Glavine and Greg Maddux, the Braves swept a three-game series, dropping the Giants' division lead to 4 1/2 games.

From there, the losses kept coming. A defeat at the hands of the Cardinals dropped the Giants into a tie with Atlanta. When they needed to win the most, the Giants lost eight straight at home to St. Louis, Pittsburgh, and the Chicago Cubs, all losing teams themselves. Now Atlanta led the division by 3 1/2 games.

As the season began to crumble, the Giants made one last run, winning eleven of their next thirteen games to catch the Braves, setting up a classic end to the season: a four-game series in Los Angeles with their greatest rivals, the Dodgers.

The Giants trailed the Braves for first place in the division by one game going into the final four games of the season. The Giants beat the Dodgers in the first game of the series 3–1. On the same day the Houston Astros beat Atlanta 10–8, leaving both teams dead-locked for first place.

The next night in Atlanta, just hours before the Giants were set to play their own game, the Braves beat Colorado 7–4. That meant the Giants knew they needed to win before stepping on the field in Los Angeles. The Dodgers scored three runs in the first inning off of John Burkett, but the great Bonds would not let his team lose. Bonds hit two home runs and a double, driving in seven runs, and the Giants came back to win 8–7 to remain tied with Atlanta.

On Saturday, Atlanta crushed Colorado 10–1, forcing the Giants to win again. They did, 5–3, leaving the final game of the season to decide it all. If both Atlanta and San Francisco won, the two teams would play a winner-takes-all one-game playoff in San Francisco the next day.

In Atlanta, the Braves won again 5–3 over Colorado to finish the season 104–58. Thus, a season that had started with the Giants thinking they would be playing in Florida continued with a summer of riveting baseball for the people of San Francisco. The Giants had already won 103 games, more than any team in baseball except for the Braves. So it all came down to one game against the Los Angeles Dodgers. The Giants had come too far, Bonds said, to lose now. The magic would continue. They would win.

They didn't.

Los Angeles ended the Giants' miracle run, beating San Francisco badly, 12–1. The Giants finished the season 103–59. It was only the third time since 1900 that a team had won one hundred games and did not make the playoffs. Only one team in baseball had won more games, but it did not matter. The Braves were division champions by one heartbreaking game, and the season was over.

Barry Bonds was named National League Most Valuable Player, hitting .336 with 46 home runs and driving in 123 runs. He had carried an entire team seemingly for the whole season. He and his team had done everything the fans could want, even though they fell short by one game.

In the end, the San Francisco Giants did not make the playoffs, but they achieved something greater: They made the people of San Francisco fall in love not only with baseball again, but with their team. The Giants again belonged to them. They weren't moving to Florida or anywhere else. It was a victory almost as sweet as the World Series, and the San Francisco love affair with their baseball team has lasted to this very day.

While it did not take the pain away from not reaching the playoffs that year, the 1993 Giants would also have a lasting impact on baseball. After the season, Major League Baseball decided a team that enjoyed such a great season deserved to make the playoffs and, for the first time, starting in 1995, they added an extra playoff spot, called the wild card, allowing a team with the second-best record in its league to qualify for the playoffs. The Giants didn't benefit that year, but they were a large part of the changes that were to come.

TOP TEN LIST

The 1993 Giants didn't win the World Series. They didn't even make the playoffs after winning 103 games. What they did do, however, was connect to their city in a way that made the victories that were to come more special. Here are ten teams that did the same for their cities, proving that winning the final game isn't always the only way to win.

1. 1953 Milwaukee Braves: Having left Boston, the Braves became beloved in Milwaukee because they were the city's first big-league team. They took on the powerhouse Dodgers and Yankees, and beat them both.

2. 1962 New York Mets: After the Giants and Dodgers left for San Francisco and Los Angeles in 1958, the National League finally returned to New York.

3. 1995 Seattle Mariners: For the first time since the team was founded in 1977, it made the playoffs.

4. 1995 Cleveland Indians: Cleveland hadn't made the playoffs since 1954—a drought of forty-one years. Until this team.

5. 1967 Boston Red Sox: After years of losing following the retirement of Ted Williams, this team went from worst to first place and returned the Red Sox to the heart of Boston.

6. 1936 New York Yankees: The first champions since Ruth. Joe DiMaggio became a star.

7. 1968 Detroit Tigers: After the five-day riots of 1967 that divided the city, baseball reunited the people.

8. 1979 Pittsburgh Pirates: The team slogan of "We Are Family" became a rallying cry for the city and helped propel the Pirates to the World Series.

9. 2013 Los Angeles Dodgers: Years of turmoil generated by a messy divorce between the co-owners of the team resulted in Commissioner Bud Selig and Major League Baseball having to take control of the Dodgers and had made the team the laughingstock of the league. With new

ownership in place and an exciting team on the field, the 2013 team made baseball fun again in Los Angeles.

10. 1985 Toronto Blue Jays: The Montreal Expos had been the first Canadian team to make the playoffs, but it was this Canadian team that turned one of the great hockey cities into baseball lovers, too.

Too Good to Be True

Mark McGwire and Sammy Sosa

o one thought it would ever happen, but in the mid-1990s, America had finally, once and for all, become sick of baseball. More accurately, America had grown sick of the fighting between the players and team owners when it came time to negotiate a new contract. Since 1972, each time a contract expired, a work stoppage had followed. There were strikes, like the first one in 1972 and the worst one in 1981, during which the players decided not to play because they did not feel they

were being treated fairly, and there were lockouts, when the owners refused to allow the players to play unless they agreed to new working conditions. The public wanted to watch their favorite sport. The players were rich. The owners were richer. They should have been able to get along.

Yet they couldn't, and the final straw came on August 12, 1994, when the players walked out—simply stopped showing up, stopped playing games—because they did not believe the team owners were working fairly with them. The owners and the commissioner believed the players were making too much money, had too much control, and they wanted some of that control back. Ownership held so firm that they did the unthinkable: instead of negotiating with the players, they shut baseball down. No more games. No pennant races. Perhaps most painful, they cancelled the World Series for the first time in nearly a hundred years. The year 1994 became known as "The Year of the Strike."

The last time a World Series had been canceled was in 1904, when the National League New York Giants refused to play the American League Boston

Americans. It was only the second-ever World Series and the event had not yet become the monumental stage that we know it as today. Millions of people weren't watching the games on TV, and millions of dollars weren't at risk.

The 1994 stoppage was infinitely worse, and not only because the sport was so much bigger in terms of popularity. Fans were smart. They knew all too well that players were making millions of dollars a year, and they knew that owners were making tens of millions of dollars a year—yet somehow the players and owners couldn't agree on how to split up all that money, so they stopped playing. There were no more games, yet the fans kept on losing. After years of forgiving baseball teams and players for the previous work stoppages, the fans finally walked away filled with anger and frustration. America's love affair with baseball was officially over.

For the next three seasons, from the time the game returned in the spring of 1995, baseball tried to rebuild its relationship with the public, one fan at a time. Cal Ripken Jr, the great Baltimore Orioles shortstop, and Tony Gwynn, the legendary right fielder for the San Diego Padres, signed autographs before and after games. The fans came to love both players even more for the gesture, but still the bitter feelings toward Major League Baseball persisted. The hurt ran deep and it showed; both stadium attendance and television ratings plummeted.

But on the first day of the 1998 season, Mark McGwire, the hulking first baseman of the St. Louis Cardinals, hit a grand slam to beat the Los Angeles Dodgers. The next day, he hit a three-run home run, and then another home run on the third day. Three days of baseball, three home runs. By the end of April, McGwire had twelve home runs and slowly, the public, though still mad at baseball, began to take notice.

McGwire had hit so many home runs, so fast, that suddenly baseball's past became part of its present, for McGwire's hot start drew comparisons to Roger Maris, the old New York Yankees right fielder who held the all-time single-season home run record of 61 home runs. It was quite possibly, along with Hank Aaron's all-time career home run record of 755, the most revered record in all of American sports.

Each day McGwire hit another home run, he captivated the nation, and people began to remember why they loved baseball so much—how hard it was to spend the summer months, when all the other sports were finished for the year, without the game they grew up with as kids.

When the home runs started flying, the fans started coming back.

The truth was that between 1994 and 1998, players had begun hitting home runs in record numbers. Babe Ruth had once hit 60 home runs in 1927, which stood as the monumental achievement in sports at the time. Sixty home runs? No one would ever break that, right? Yet Maris, with the odds against him, broke the record in 1961. 61 homers in '61.

The new record would stand for decades, as a home run drought persisted from 1962 until 1993. Even getting to 50 home runs was considered a massive achievement during that period. All told, in the 76 years between 1927, when Ruth hit 60, and 1993, the year before the strike, only nine players had ever hit more than 50 homers in a season.

Now, suddenly, everyone was doing it. In 1994, Matt Williams, the Giants' third baseman, had hit 43

home runs by August 12, the day the season ended
due to the strike. He never had the chance to hit more
that season, and so the record of 61 stood firm yet another year. In 1995, Albert Belle of Cleveland led the
league by hitting 50 home runs. In 1996, Baltimore's
Brady Anderson, who had never hit more than 11
home runs in any previous season, hit 50. McGwire,
then playing for the Oakland A's, hit 52 that same
season. In 1997, another slugger, Seattle's Ken Griffey
Jr., hit 56 homers. McGwire, traded midseason to St.
Louis, hit 58 that year.

What in the world was going on?

Many people in the game believed the reason was
simply that players were bigger, faster, and stronger.
They made so much money they could afford to keep
in shape year-round. They didn't have to work odd
jobs in the off-season, as the lower-paid stars of the
past had. And they were so rich they could afford
nutritionists who taught them to eat better, and personal chefs and trainers to keep them fit in ways that
players of the past had never dreamed possible.

Whatever the reason, baseball fans certainly
loved the results, and the media noticed. On May 25

of 1998, McGwire hit another home run, this time against Colorado. It was his twenty-fifth of the year and the sports writers began calculating his chances of breaking Maris's record.

None of the attention made McGwire happy. He was a big man, six-foot-five, 250 pounds, but was uncomfortable in the public spotlight. In turn, McGwire's discomfort with being the star of the moment made Bud Selig, the commissioner of baseball, unhappy too. Here was baseball with a wonderful opportunity to win back its fans after a bitter work stoppage with a moment that happens once in a lifetime, and the star of the show, Mark McGwire, acted as though he wanted to be anywhere else in the world when the game needed him.

On the same day that McGwire hit his twenty-fifth homer, Sammy Sosa, the talented but frustrating right fielder of the Chicago Cubs, hit two home runs against Atlanta. McGwire had 25 home runs. Sosa had just hit his eleventh and twelfth of the year—a long way from McGwire's total. But what followed was one of the greatest home run tears—and one of the greatest competitions—ever.

The Philadelphia Phillies came to town. Sosa hit two home runs.

The Cubs played the Florida Marlins. Sosa hit two more home runs.

The Cubs played three games against Sosa's old team, the Chicago White Sox, and Sosa hit a home run in each game.

During one five-game stretch, Sosa had blasted one out of the park in every game.

Over 33 days, Sosa would hit 21 home runs. At the All-Star break, McGwire had 37 home runs, Sosa 33. First it was one guy chasing history. Now there were two! And America had taken notice. Attendance in ballparks was up, as were TV ratings.

Baseball was back!

But there was more: Unlike McGwire, Sosa loved the spotlight. He began his career with the Texas Rangers, but they quickly gave up on him. As did his second team, the Chicago White Sox, who traded him to the Cubs. He was obviously a talented player who frustrated fans and teams because it was clear how much better he could be. He had already shown glimpses of his ability to run and hit for power, hitting 30 home runs and stealing 30 bases in 1995, and now, with his sudden explosion of power, Sosa was on the verge of becoming a star and was determined to enjoy every minute of it.

While McGwire frowned, Sosa had fun. After a home run swing, he did a little hop out of the batter's box that the TV cameras showed every time. When he reached the dugout, the camera would follow him and he would blow kisses and flash peace signs to the fans, gestures that became as famous as Sosa himself. People loved it.

With Sosa sharing the attention, even McGwire started to enjoy the moment a little bit more. Sosa made him laugh, reminded him that baseball, after all, was supposed to be fun, and why not laugh? The whole world was watching this two-man home run show.

One day, Steve Wilstein, a reporter with the Associated Press, noticed a bottle of pills in McGwire's locker and asked him what they were. The pills were called androstenedione and they were considered to have similar effects to steroids. In other words, they helped a player increase his strength and even heal faster from injury. The pills were banned in other sports, but not in baseball. McGwire said he used "andro," as the pills were called, but said he never used steroids. Using steroids would be cheating, and McGwire said he never cheated.

For the rest of the summer, the McGwire-Sosa home run chase dominated the conversation about baseball as it captivated the country. It felt like each day McGwire would hit one, Sosa would follow with a home run of his own. The memory of the 1994 strike was being replaced with the kind of baseball chatter that is usually reserved for September, when every game is a must-win . . .

Did Sammy hit one?

Did McGwire hit one?

By mid-August, it seemed a foregone conclusion that *both* players would pass Maris's record of 61. Television news programs had begun cutting away from their broadcasts to show both players each time they came to bat.

On August 31, with the Cincinnati Reds in town, Sosa hit home run number 55 and caught McGwire for the first time all season. With four weeks left in the season, and both only six home runs away from tying Maris, the pair was dead even.

It didn't take long from there. On September 7, just one week later, McGwire reached the all-time home run record of 61, beating Sosa to the prize. Then, one day later, with McGwire's Cardinals playing Sosa's Cubs in St. Louis, the magical moment occurred in the fourth inning. TV networks all over the country were tuned in. Pitcher Steve Trachsel delivered a fastball down in the strike zone. McGwire crushed it, hitting a line drive that just reached over the left field fence.

The umpires stopped the game while the crowd cheered wildly. Waiting to greet McGwire at home plate, in addition to the entire Cardinals team, was his son, Matt, holding the bat that had just hit the record-breaking homer. McGwire lifted him up in the air as flashbulbs popped throughout the crowd. Sosa raced in from right field and hugged McGwire. McGwire had done it. He had passed a record that had stood for thirty-seven years.

And there were still three weeks left in the season!

Sosa, too, passed Maris, four days later, making it the first time in baseball history that two players passed the single-season home run record in the same year. For a moment, on September 25, Sosa even passed McGwire, leading 66 home runs to 65. Later that night, though, McGwire hit one of his own to tie things up again.

Sosa wouldn't hit another home run for the rest of the year, finishing with 66. McGwire would go on a final tear to hit two on September 26, another on the 27th, and on the last day of the season, September 28, McGwire hit his last home run of the year off Carl Pavano of the Montreal Expos. His 70th of the year.

Seventy home runs!

McGwire had become a national hero.

The next year, for an encore, Sosa and McGwire did it again! Both surpassed Maris's mark of 61 for the second straight year. No one in baseball history—not Ruth, not Mantle, not DiMaggio, not Mays—had ever hit 60 home runs in consecutive years, and now both guys were doing it again. McGwire won this race, too, hitting 65 home runs to Sosa's 63.

Baseball hadn't just returned. It had returned to the center of the American heart in a way it hadn't in decades. The excitement that surrounded the summer of McGwire and Sosa served as a reminder that once again, when played at its best, highest level, America loved baseball in a more passionate, personal way than any other sport.

The summer of 1998, however, was also too good to be true. It was soon revealed that many players had been using illegal drugs to enhance their performance. The players at first denied it, but the truth eventually came to light. The fans who had cheered on this magical season and given their heart back to baseball felt cheated, tricked. In the eyes of not only the public, but of the media, the government, and law enforcement, one of the most important records in baseball history had been broken by cheaters. The consequences would once again devastate the sport.

For years afterward, the battle against performance-enhancing drugs made as many headlines as the players did themselves. Fans didn't know whom to trust anymore.

As for McGwire, he thought his record would stand for a long time, but Barry Bonds, who also would one day admit that he used illegal drugs (though he would say he did so unknowingly), hit 73 home runs just three years later. By this point, fans no longer believed what they were watching, even though they still attended games in record numbers.

McGwire returned to baseball in 2010 as a hitting coach for the Cardinals, but on the condition that he admit he used steroids, including during the 1998 season. On national television, McGwire did just that and said he hoped the fans could somehow forgive him. He was permitted to work for the Cardinals and later the Los Angeles Dodgers, but he is rarely viewed as a hero anymore. Despite his great accomplishments on the field, he has yet to be elected to the Hall of Fame, and may never be.

The price for 1998 would be enormous. Instead of cheers, baseball would treat 1998 as though it never happened. Over his career, Sammy Sosa would hit 609 home runs. In 2001, he became the only man in history of baseball to hit 60 home runs three times, when he hit 64, but when he retired in 2007, he would leave the game with no connection to it or the Chicago Cubs. He, too, came nowhere close to being voted into the Baseball Hall of Fame.

Perhaps the best example of how differently people would look at what was supposed to be the greatest year in the history of baseball is that the sport itself rarely, if ever, mentions that momentous chase in 1998 for the record. That year was proof that there is no substitute for hard work, and nothing—not even millions of people cheering and billions of dollars earned by the players, owners, and the league—is as important, in the long run, as a person's reputation.

McGwire–Sosa

TOP TEN LIST

The Mark McGwire–Sammy Sosa home run chase simultaneously revived baseball while becoming a turning point in sports regarding the prevalence of performance-enhancing drugs. The record books would change as well as baseball itself. Here is a list of the all-time single-season home run leaders.

1. Barry Bonds—73 (2001)
2. Mark McGwire—70 (1998)
3. Sammy Sosa—66 (1998)
4. Mark McGwire—65 (1999)
5. Sammy Sosa—64 (2001)
6. Sammy Sosa—63 (1999)
7. Roger Maris—61 (1961)
8. Babe Ruth—60 (1927)
9. Babe Ruth—59 (1921)
10. (tie) Hank Greenberg—58 (1938) / Jimmie Foxx (1932) / Mark McGwire (1997) / Ryan Howard (2006)

Victory Summer

THE 1998 NEW YORK YANKEES

On Monday April 6, 1998, panic struck the heart of New York City.

The Yankees had lost their first two games of the season.

People went nuts. There were 160 games left, but the season was obviously over because *the Yankees were 0 and 2.*

These were the Yankees of George Steinbrenner, who spent millions upon millions of dollars each season to ensure his team won. The Yankees, who had won 96 games the previous season and 92 the season before. Winning and reaching the playoffs wasn't just expected, it was *demanded*.

Yet they lost again and were 0–3.

After a win and another loss, an 8–0 beatdown by the Mariners, they were 1–4.

The April 7 *New York Times* headline screamed.

"YANKS SLIDE CONTINUES."

Nothing seemed to work. When the pitchers struggled, the Yankees got creamed. When they pitched well, the hitters didn't hit. When there were runners finally on base, the star players like Bernie Williams, Tino Martinez and Paul O'Neill couldn't get that clutch hit that would score runs. Making matters worse, in the 8–0 loss to the Mariners, not only did Seattle superstar Alex Rodriguez hit a home run off Andy Pettitte, but later in the game, the Yankees' best relief pitcher, Mariano Rivera, got hurt and would miss the next two weeks. Everything that could have gone wrong to start the season *did* go wrong. And it sent fans wringing their hands in dread.

It wasn't just that the Yankees were supposed to

win, but that 1998 was supposed to be the year they rebounded from the heartbreaking way the 1997 season had ended. The Yankees had won the World Series in 1996 for the first time in eighteen years and, in 1997, fully expected to repeat as champions. Despite those ninety-six wins, they had played a very dangerous, very talented Cleveland team in the playoffs, and Rivera had given up a home run to Sandy Alomar in the eighth inning of the deciding fifth game. The season, suddenly, was over. This year was supposed to make up for the disappointment and restore the team to the top.

Yet now they could barely win a game.

When you lose game after game, you hope that eventually something, *anything* good will happen. A day after their 8–0 loss, the Yankees and Mariners played again. Jim Bullinger threw his second pitch of the game and Chuck Knoblauch, the Yankees' second baseman, hit a home run. Then the talented young shortstop, Derek Jeter, doubled. O'Neill continued the rally with a double of his own. Tino Martinez hit a single, then Darryl Strawberry hit a home run, and Jorge Posada hit *another* home run. Before the very first inning was over, the Yankees led 6–0.

They won that game, and just like that, things were looking up. "When you lose," manager Joe Torre said, "you don't think too big. You just want to win a game, just one game."

But it wasn't just one game. They won again the next day, and the day after.

And then the next.

After two more wins in Detroit, it was eight in a row.

And now, the team that couldn't win suddenly couldn't lose.

By May 21, the Yankees were 31–9. They had won 30 of their last 35 games, but it wasn't just the winning, it was the magic that lived within the winning. On May 17, David Wells took the mound against Minnesota. He faced twenty-seven Minnesota Twins batters, and got all twenty-seven out in a row. Nobody reached base. No hits. No walks. No wild pitches and no errors by his defense. It was the first time in the ninety-five-year history of the Yankees that a pitcher threw a perfect game during the regular season.

New York is a big place, eight million people strong, with so many people from so many different places. There are tall buildings throughout the world, but no other city is filled with giant skyscrapers quite like New York. The personalities of the Yankees were just as big. There was right fielder Paul O'Neill, the tall kid from Ohio with a bad temper, who smashed the water cooler with his bat when he was frustrated, but played to win every day. There was Derek Jeter, the rising superstar, who as a little kid had said he wanted to play shortstop for the Yankees when he grew up—and then was so good he actually made it happen. There was Bernie Williams, the center fielder from Puerto Rico, who could hit both right-handed and left-handed, and was also an excellent guitar player. There was Darryl Strawberry, all six-foot-six of him, who hit baseballs so far they looked like they'd land on the moon. There were the fearless and carefree starting pitchers, David Wells and David Cone.

And then there was Orlando "El Duque" Hernandez, who had come to the Yankees after escaping his home-land of Cuba on a small boat, hoping to pitch in the Major Leagues. Hernandez was a star pitcher in Cuba, but was accused of being disloyal for refusing to give the government information on a teammate who had previously left the country. Once a national hero, he had been prohibited from playing baseball by the country's dictator, Fidel Castro. Fearing for his future, he left the country, too, for America.

The leader of the team was the manager, Joe Torre, who had begun his major league playing career in 1960. He had been a nine-time all-star, had played alongside legends like Hank Aaron and Eddie Mathews and Bob Gibson, had won an MVP Award as a player, but had never won a World Series title until 1996 with the Yankees. Even Torre was a beloved celebrity in New York.

Each of the key players on the team may have come from a different place, but they all had one thing in common: Each was so tough-minded that, together, the Yankees were a fearsome team to play.

The funny thing was, for all of the winning, the Yankees in 1998 weren't even the biggest story in baseball. That title belonged to Mark McGwire and Sammy Sosa, who seemed to be hitting home runs every day, chasing the single-season home run record of 61, set by Roger Maris in 1961. While McGwire and Sosa captivated the nation, the Yankees, almost quietly, just kept winning.

At the All-Star break, the Yankees were easily in first place in the American League East, with an eleven-game lead over the Red Sox. A month later, the lead was twenty games. They went into Kansas City and Tim Raines, Tino Martinez, and Bernie Williams all hit home runs. The Yankees won 7–1, and their record was a staggering 91–30.

This type of winning, it should be noted, almost never happens in baseball. The reason is the game it-self—how difficult it is for an entire team to be consis-tently good. Unlike the star of a basketball or football team, the best pitcher on a baseball team doesn't pitch every day. It's difficult for any one player to take over an entire game, day after day, the way a LeBron James or a rifle-armed quarterback like Peyton Manning can.

They won their one hundredth game of the season on September 4, the fastest team ever to win a hun-dred games in baseball history. By the time the season ended, the Yankees were 114–48, the most wins in American League history, breaking Cleveland's 1954 record and second only to the 1906 Chicago Cubs, who won 116 games. It was a summer of winning.

When the playoffs began, however, the Yankees

were tense. Brian Cashman, the Yankees' general manager, was so nervous he thought he would go crazy. Everything thus far had worked: Bernie Williams had won the batting title, hitting .339. Jeter hit .324, scored 127 runs, and stole 30 bases. Cone won 20 games. Rivera proved he could stand the pressure of being the closer. His 1.91 ERA was so small you needed a microscope to see it. El Duque was a fantastic surprise, so good and so fearless he even stared down and beat the great Pedro Martinez, who was the best pitcher in baseball at the time, in a classic Red Sox–Yankees duel at Yankee Stadium.

Everything was great—and that made Cashman feel even worse, because now they *had* to win the World Series. Anything less and that amazing season—all those wins—would be forgotten in a giant wave of disappointment.

Cashman was so anxious about the Yankees' situation that it brought up an interesting question: Is it worse to have a terrible season with no chance of winning, or to have one of the greatest seasons of all time, win all summer long, and then not win the championship?

It wasn't just Cashman who had such thoughts. Jeter would say that failing to win the championship made a season a failure. Sure, the Yankees had won all summer, but another team could get hot. Or his team could get cold at the worst possible time. One opposing pitcher, like Martinez if they played the Red Sox, could have the game of his life. What if the ball went through Knoblauch's legs in the ninth inning of a tie game? What if the umpires made a bad call that cost them a game? What if Jeter got hurt or if Mariano wasn't perfect when he needed to be?

Cashman was nervous, but it wasn't like he didn't have a reason to be. There were other great teams who had mashed everybody in the regular season, then lost in the playoffs and ended up forgotten over time. The 1954 Cleveland Indians had won 111 games but were swept in the World Series by Willie Mays and the Giants. The 109-win Baltimore Orioles lost the World Series in five games to the "Miracle" Mets in 1969, one of the great upsets of all time. The 1953 Brooklyn Dodgers had Jackie Robinson, won 105 games, but lost to the Yankees in the World Series. The 1946 Red Sox had Ted Williams, won 104 games, but lost the World Series to the St. Louis Cardinals.

And the team that won the most games of all time, those 1906 Chicago Cubs from so long ago? What happened to them? They won 116 games and lost the World Series to the Chicago White Sox.

It happened. Would it also happen to the Yankees?

At first, it didn't seem so. In the first round of the playoffs, the Yankees blitzed through Texas in three straight games and then met the dreaded Cleveland Indians in the American League Championship Series—the rematch they'd waited for all year. The Yankees crushed the Indians in the first game of the American League Championship Series—and then, in Game 2, the unthinkable happened . . .

Tied 1–1 in the twelfth inning with a man on first, Tino Martinez fielded a bunt by Travis Fryman and turned to throw to first. Fryman, running to first, was in the way. Martinez's throw hit Fryman in the back and rolled away. The Yankees thought Fryman should have been called out for interfering with Martinez's throw—but he wasn't. Meanwhile, Enrique Wilson, who had been on first, kept running and running while the Yankees were complaining and complaining. By the time Knoblauch finally picked up the ball, Cleveland had already scored the go-ahead run. They would score twice more and win 4–1 to tie the series. Then the Indians went to Cleveland and won again in Game 3. All of a sudden, the Indians needed just two more wins to end the Yankees' season for the second straight year—and had the next two games at home to do it. All of the Yankees' fears were coming true: the bad call, the unlucky bounce, now put them behind two games to one to a team that did not fear them.

The whole season now sat on the shoulders of Orlando Hernandez, a pitcher who hadn't even been with the team when the season started. The pressure was enormous, and El Duque responded by hanging out with the waiters and waitresses at the restaurant in the Yankees' hotel in Cleveland, just to speak Spanish because it reminded him of being home. The rest of the Yankees wondered if Hernandez knew how big a game he was pitching. In the United States, pitchers don't even talk to their own teammates much on the day they pitch, and here this guy was, doing dishes at the hotel!

When the game started, the fiery O'Neill homered in the first inning to give the Yankees an early lead. In the bottom of the inning, with two outs, Jim

Thome, the Cleveland slugger whose arms and legs looked as large as tree trunks, hit a ball so hard it appeared it would wind up in the Atlantic Ocean. O'Neill stood and watched the ball sail toward him, on its way out of the stadium. It was a sure home run, Thome thought, and he continued what he expected to be a home run trot—when suddenly . . . suddenly . . . the wind caught the ball and began to bring it back into the stadium . . . and into O'Neill's glove for the final out of the inning. To this day, Thome *still* doesn't know how that ball he hit wasn't a home run!

That one play seemed to change the tide.

For the rest of the game, El Duque shut down Cleveland. The Yankees won the game 4–0. When it was over, Torre said it was the hard life lessons that Hernandez had endured—facing prison if he did not tell on his friends, facing death in the ocean all those nights on a little raft escaping Cuba—that allowed him not to be scared or worried about pitching in such a big game. "When you've been through what he's been through," Torre said, "this is just a baseball game."

The Yankees wouldn't lose again for the rest of the

season. After having their revenge against the Indians, they went on to destroy the San Diego Padres in four straight games to win the World Series.

As time would pass, scandal eroded much of that magical 1998 season. Instead of remembering the great McGwire and the joyous Sosa, both would have their names linked to steroids and cheating rather than record breaking. The great home run chase that made so many people fall in love with baseball again turned out to be a moment fans would remember with regret and shame.

One aspect of that season did endure, however, and it was the historic performance of the New York Yankees. When the year finally ended, the team had played 175 games and won 125 of them, including the most important game—the last one. No team has won as much since and none may again for a very, very long time. If ever.

The 1998 New York Yankees

TOP TEN LIST

Mariano Rivera saved three out of the four wins in the Yankees' World Series sweep of the Padres. He would go on to become arguably the greatest relief pitcher of all time. Here are the all-time leaders in saves:

1. Mariano Rivera, 652
2. Trevor Hoffman, 601
3. Lee Smith, 478
4. John Franco, 424
5. Billy Wagner, 422
6. Dennis Eckersley, 390
7. Jeff Reardon, 367
8. Joe Nathan, 365
9. Troy Percival, 358
10. Randy Myers, 347

Goliath Falls

~~~~~~

The 1960 World Series

The 1960 World Series between the New York Yankees and Pittsburgh Pirates was supposed to be over before it started. Between 1947 and 1959, the Yankees appeared in the World Series ten out of thirteen years, and seven times they emerged as champions. They had the big names like Mickey Mantle, the power-hitting outfielder who could hit from both sides of the plate; the renowned slugger Roger Maris; the great catcher-turned-outfielder Yogi Berra; and the unflappable pitcher Whitey Ford, the winningest pitcher in World Series history. Ford, Berra, and Mantle would wind up in the Baseball Hall of Fame. Maris would break Babe Ruth's hallowed 1927 record of 60 home runs the following year, which would be another year the Yankees won the World Series (for good measure, they won it *again* in 1962). The Yankees had been in the World Series so many times it felt as though they had invented it.

The Yankees dominated the American League with such force that it sometimes felt like they were the only team around. In the twenty-five years from 1936 to 1960, only two other American League teams besides the Yankees had won the World Series. One was the 1945 Detroit Tigers, the other the 1948 Cleveland Indians.

What chance, then, could the Pirates have against such an unbeatable machine? The Pirates hadn't won the World Series since 1925, and hadn't even been in the World Series since 1927, when Babe Ruth and (guess who?) the rest of the Yankees destroyed them in four straight games. During those thirty-three years away from the spotlight, with only eight teams in the National League, the Pirates had finished in fourth place or worse *twenty-five times*. Not good.

So what happened in the 1960 World Series? The Yankees dominated in almost every statistical category. In three of their wins, they outscored Pittsburgh by a combined total of 38–3. Whitey Ford pitched two shutouts. The Yankees hit 10 homers and scored 55 runs in all, averaging nearly eight runs a game. They hit .338 as a team and Bobby Richardson, the Yankees' second baseman, was named the MVP of the series.

But who won?

The Pirates, that's who, and for fifty years since, people have been scratching their heads wondering how such a miraculous thing could have ever occurred.

It was the craziest of World Series. The Pirates hit only .256, yet they found a way to make every hit count. Despite getting blown out by scores of 16–3, 10–0, and 12–0 in games they lost, they won the low-scoring games and they won when it mattered most.

This series would go down in history for the stunning, bizarre, incredible way they won the seventh and deciding game in Pittsburgh at Forbes Field.

After two innings, in the winner-takes-all finale, the Pirates led 4–0. This game would definitely not be a blowout—at least not for the Yankees. Soon the good citizens of Pittsburgh would be dancing in the streets, right?

Wrong.

The Yankees began their comeback with one run in the fifth inning, and then in the sixth, after a single and a walk, Mickey Mantle hit a run-scoring single. Right after Mantle, Yogi Berra came to the plate with two men on base and launched a long home run, giving the Yankees a 5–4 lead. In the eighth, an RBI single by Johnny Blanchard and an RBI double by Clete Boyer gave the Yankees two more runs and a 7–4 lead.

With six outs left in their season, the Pirates were down 7–4 against the most powerful team in baseball. Somehow, the Yankees had done it again, down 4–0 only to score seven unanswered runs and now take the lead. It was over, right?

Wrong.

In the bottom of the eighth, the Pirates scored five runs, one of which came with two outs on a run-scoring single by 25-year old rising star Roberto Clemente, and three more on a two-out, three-run home run by little-known catcher Hal Smith. Pittsburgh had come back, and now the Pirates led 9–7 going into the top of the ninth.

The Pirates were just three outs away from the championship! *Now* Pirate fans could feel confident, right?

Wrong.

Sure enough, Mantle and Berra came through again, both driving in runs to tie the game at 9–9!

For the bottom of the ninth, the Yankees' legendary manager Casey Stengel called on Ralph Terry to pitch. Bill Mazeroski, the eighth hitter in the Pirates' order, had gone 1 for 3 and scored a run. After hitting a homer in Game 1, which the Pirates had won, he stood in the batter's box in a crazy game with the whole season on the line and a chance to win it all with one swing of the bat.

Terry threw him a fastball with the first pitch. Mazeroski watched it go by for a ball. He stepped out of the box, took a deep breath, and stepped in again. The next pitch was a slider. Mazeroski swung and connected.

The ball headed high and sharply to left field, where Berra tracked it. Berra ran back and back and stopped at the ivy-covered fence. There was no more room and nothing to do but watch as the ball cleared the wall for a home run.

The Pirates, who had been outscored, outslugged, and beaten by the mighty Yankees so badly in three games, were now world champions. Mazeroski skipped around the bases with a huge smile on his face as fans ran onto the field, wanting to touch the hero as he rounded the bases for home. His teammates waited for him at home plate.

It was arguably the greatest moment in Pittsburgh sports history. For the first time, a World Series had ended on a home run, and to this day, Mazeroski's homer remains one of the most famous moments in baseball's long and fantastic history. The Yankees had hit ten home runs in the series, the Pirates only four. Yet it was Pittsburgh who hit the one that the baseball world would always remember, the one Bill Mazeroski would never forget.

The 1960 World Series

TOP TEN LIST

Bill Mazeroski's home run in 1960 is still the only one to end the World Series in Game 7, but it wasn't the last of many spectacular fantastic finishes to the World Series. Here are ten more . . .

1. 1993, Game 6, bottom of the ninth: Toronto's Joe Carter hits a game-winning three-run homer off Mitch Williams to give the Blue Jays the World Series over Philadelphia.

2. 1926, Game 7, bottom of the ninth: Trailing 3–2 to St. Louis, Babe Ruth is thrown out trying to steal second and the Yankees lose the World Series.

3. 2001, Game 7, bottom of the ninth: Luis Gonzalez of Arizona hits a broken-bat single over the head of Derek Jeter and the Diamondbacks beat the Yankees for their first-ever championship.

4. 1955, Game 7: Johnny Podres shuts out the Yankees, 2–0. The Brooklyn Dodgers win their one and only title.

5. 1946, Game 7, bottom of the eighth: In a 3–3 game, the Cardinals' Enos Slaughter races home all the way from first on a double to beat the Red Sox.

6. 1991, Game 7: Twins' Jack Morris pitches a complete-game ten-inning 1–0 win vs. Braves.

7. 1953, Game 6: Yankees' Billy Martin singles in the bottom of the ninth to beat the Dodgers and win the championship.

8. 1997, Game 7: Florida's Edgar Renteria singles in the bottom of the eleventh to beat Cleveland. The Marlins win their first World Series title.

9. 1962, Game 7: Bobby Richardson snares Willie McCovey's game-ending line drive and the Yankees beat San Francisco.

10. 1924, Game 7: Earl McNeely doubles to left in the bottom of the twelfth against the New York Giants to give the Washington Senators their only World Series championship.

Something to Prove

ROBERTO CLEMENTE'S
QUEST

n the 1950s and 1960s, baseball was a very
crowded place. As already noted, the Yankees
owned the better part of both decades, appearing
in the World Series thirteen times in those twenty
years, winning eight championships. New York baseball in general dominated the 1950s, as a New York
team—the Yankees, Dodgers, or Giants—appeared in
the World Series every year between 1949 and 1958.

The game finally went transcontinental. The
Giants and Dodgers left New York in 1958, moving

from Harlem and Brooklyn to San Francisco and Los Angeles, respectively, and for the first time since the late 1800s, baseball relocated and expanded to new cities: The Houston Colt .45s (now the Astros), Los Angeles Angels, Kansas City Royals, and Montreal Expos, among others, were born.

The level of superstar talent in the game was as full as a Thanksgiving Day table.

The 1951 World Series featured two rookies—Willie Mays and Mickey Mantle—who would dominate the next two decades as the most dynamic players in their league, as well as two timeless veterans, Joe DiMaggio and Yogi Berra. Jackie Robinson was not just a superstar but an inspirational symbol for fans everywhere. Roy Campanella wasn't just the best catcher in the National League for years—he was a three-time Most Valuable Player. In 1954, the great Hank Aaron arrived, and even he couldn't match Stan Musial as the best hitter in the National League. The end of the 1950s saw a power-hitting shortstop, Ernie Banks of the Cubs, win the NL MVP Award twice in a row—in 1958 and 1959. In the American League, Ted Williams, the last man to hit .400, was still the leader of the Red Sox, and the best hitter in the game.

The 1960s were just as loaded with stars. Before the change was made to increase the size of the strike zone, Roger Maris and Mickey Mantle chased Babe Ruth's single-season home run record, and a young outfielder named Frank Robinson would become the only player to win the MVP Award as a member of both the American and the National Leagues. After the change to the strike zone, great pitching seemed to dominate the game and the mound belonged to two of the all-time best: Bob Gibson and Sandy Koufax.

With so little room to be noticed, and with so many big stars elbowing for a bigger place on stage, Roberto Clemente often felt forgotten.

Since the late 1950s, after he was given a chance by the Pittsburgh Pirates, who drafted him off of a Brooklyn Dodgers minor league team, Clemente had enjoyed a tremendous following of fans who loved his electric, slashing style of play.

Clemente was the kind of ballplayer who did everything right, and he did it dangerously, but most important, when Clemente played, fans always expected something breathtaking to happen. When he hit, the ball would rip off of his bat low and flat, whistle through the infield, and crash into the outfield gaps. He was not a home run hitter like Frank Robinson or Aaron, but many times—240 times over his career—those line drives would cut through the air and sail over the fence.

When Clemente ran the bases, it wasn't just with his legs, but with his arms, with his teeth clenched, his whole body lurching and reaching for his destination. When he threw from the outfield, the ball resembled a comet, a bullet, a rocket. A batter would single into a gap in the outfield, hungry to turn the hit into a double, but Clemente would field the ball and fire it into the infield, causing the runner to retreat back to first or risk being gunned down at second by a perfect throw.

Most fun for Clemente was when a runner on first would try to take third on a base hit to right field. Then he could really let loose a big throw, erasing his challenger at third. The crowd would buzz. Clemente could do something few players in history could do: He made defense as exciting as offense. As if to emphasize the point, he won twelve straight Gold Glove Awards.

Clemente was all these things and something else, too: dark-skinned as if he were African American, yet born and raised in Puerto Rico, Clemente was baseball's first Latin American superstar. He was the game's first internationally recognizable figure, not just for his baseball fame, but also for being a symbol of success and humanity to baseball fans in places such as Cuba, Venezuela, and Nicaragua. Clemente responded to his connection to Latino fans and their countries by giving more of himself: by trying to help poorer countries through raising money and promoting charity.

It also meant having to conduct interviews in English, a second language for Clemente, when most American sportswriters not only did not speak Spanish (most still don't today), but many also found Clemente's struggle with English a source of ridicule.

It meant having pride in being Puerto Rican while trying to make American baseball fans feel comfortable. For years, Roberto would go by the American nickname "Bobby" as an attempt to connect better with English-speaking baseball fans. Yet for all the fans who loved him, Roberto often felt as though he was not quite as accepted as stars like Mickey Mantle or Willie Mays.

On the field, Clemente also felt slighted, because for all of his greatness, the national media focused on other players. In 1960, he led the Pirates to the World Series against the Yankees, and the Pirates upset the mighty Yanks in seven games—but that series would always and only be remembered for Bill Mazeroski's home run in the bottom of the ninth of Game 7. Clemente led the National League in batting average four times, in 1961, 1964, 1965, and 1967. He led both leagues in hits twice. He piled up more than two hundred hits a season in four different years. He won the MVP Award in 1966. And of course, there were those twelve straight Gold Glove Awards. Yet Clemente played right field at the same time as two other all-time superstars in the National League: Henry Aaron and Frank Robinson. Aaron and Robinson seemed to generate the most headlines because of their prowess as power hitters.

So in 1971, with the Pirates playing the mighty defending champion Baltimore Orioles in the World Series, Clemente made sure to take advantage of the opportunity to be on the big stage to prove that he was in the same class as the great ones, to ensure that no one would ever forget him.

He'd already put together a fantastic playoff performance, having hit .333 in Pittsburgh's four-game win over San Francisco in the National League Championship Series, but he was even hotter in the World Series. Clemente went 2 for 4 with a double in the first game and 2 for 5 with a double in the second, but the Pirates lost both games in Baltimore. When the series shifted to Pittsburgh, the Pirates won the next three games and Clemente had at least one hit in each game, including going 3 for 4 in Game 4. The Pirates were a game away from winning the World Series and Clemente had 8 hits in 17 at-bats—a .471 batting average.

In Game 6, with the Pirates needing a win for the championship and the Orioles needing a win to force a winner-takes-all final game, Clemente hit a triple off Jim Palmer in the first inning and then gave the Pirates the lead in the third with a home run to right field.

The Orioles would come back to win that game in the bottom of the tenth inning, leading to a series-deciding seventh game. Clemente had but one hit in Game 7, yet it was a home run in the fourth inning that gave the Pirates the lead. The Pirates would go on to win the game and the second World Series of Clemente's career. Clemente, having hit .414 with two home runs, was named Most Valuable Player, the first Latin American to ever win the award.

After the game he spoke on national television in Spanish and English, making him an even greater hero in his homeland of Puerto Rico, not to mention to kids in the Caribbean and Mexico.

The next year, on the final day of the 1972 season, Clemente recorded his three-thousandth hit—a milestone that to this day is used as a measuring stick for a Hall of Fame career. Unfortunately, it would be the final hit of Clemente's career.

During Christmas of that year, a terrible earthquake struck Nicaragua. Clemente organized a mission to bring first aid and other supplies to the victims. On December 31 another great tragedy occurred, when Clemente's plane carrying emergency supplies to Nicaragua crashed into the Atlantic Ocean shortly after takeoff. His body was never recovered.

Baseball still honors Clemente's commitment to others by awarding the Roberto Clemente Award each season to the player who "best exemplifies the game of baseball, sportsmanship, community involvement and the individual's contribution to his team."

For all the years when he did not think he was recognized as the great player he was, Roberto Clemente would never have to worry about being forgotten. His greatness would be in his ability to inspire baseball fans and generations of future players both with his play on the baseball field and with his selfless humanity off of it.

TOP TEN LIST

It doesn't always happen, but the World Series is the ultimate stage for the best players to be great. Roberto Clemente used the 1971 World Series to show the public his talents. Other Hall of Fame players (and soon-to-be Hall of Famers) have followed, saving their best for the last series of the year, the World Series.

1. Hank Aaron, 1957: Hit .393, 3 HR against Yankees

2. Babe Ruth, 1928: Hit .625, 3 HR against Cardinals

3. Reggie Jackson, 1977: Hit .450, 5 HR against Dodgers

4. Bob Gibson, 1967: 3–0, 1.00 ERA, 26 K against Red Sox

5. Willie Stargell, 1979: Hit .400, 4 2B, 3 HR against Orioles

6. Sandy Koufax, 1965: 2–1, 0.38 ERA. Pitched 2-hit shutout in Game 7 against Twins

7. Brooks Robinson, 1970: Spectacular defense,
   hit .429 average against Reds

8. Derek Jeter, 2000: Hit .409, 2 HR against Mets

9. Lou Gehrig, 1932: Hit .529, 3 HR, 8 RBI against
   Cubs

10. Madison Bumgarner, 2014: 2-0, 1 SV, 0.43 ERA,
    21 IP, 17K against Royals

The Best Ever

The 1975 World Series

Even today, in a different century, people still think the 1975 World Series was better than the rest, better than all the ones that came before it, even the ones that had Babe Ruth, Lou Gehrig, Willie Mays, and Joe DiMaggio in them, and better than the ones that came after, with Derek Jeter and Reggie Jackson, David Ortiz and Albert Pujols. Some historians may think the 1912 Red Sox–Giants classic was best. Others may point to the 1947 Yankees–Dodgers showdown. Today's baseball fans may prefer the 1991 Twins–Braves World Series, the 1993 Phillies–Blue Jays, the 2002 Giants–Angels, or the

2011 Cardinals–Rangers. Everyone is entitled to their opinions.

It is one thing, however, to talk about a game or a player or a series as "the best ever," and quite another to explain why a certain series was so special. As for the thriller between the Cincinnati Reds and the Boston Red Sox, here are just a few reasons why, decades later, people still talk about the 1975 World Series:

1. Two games were decided in extra innings.
2. Two more games were decided in the ninth inning.
3. Six of the seven games were won by a team who had to come from behind.
4. In one game, the winning team came from behind twice.
5. The Reds had won 108 games in 1975 and were considered one of the greatest teams of all time, "The Big Red Machine."
6. The Red Sox were one of the best young teams, primed to be dominant for years.
7. Combined, the two teams fielded five future Hall

of Fame players: Carl Yastrzemski and Carlton
Fisk of the Red Sox; Johnny Bench, Joe Morgan,
and Tony Perez of Cincinnati. Sparky Anderson,
the Reds' manager, would also make the Hall of
Fame. Boston's Jim Rice, who would one day also
make the Hall of Fame, missed the series with
an injured wrist, and another Hall of Fame–level
player, Pete Rose—baseball's all-time leader in
hits—would not be allowed entry into the Hall of
Fame because he was caught betting on baseball.
In total, eight Hall of Fame talents from just two
teams.

8. Game 6, widely considered the greatest playoff
game ever played, also featured one of the game's
most famous moments: Carlton Fisk's dramatic
twelfth inning, game-winning home run off the
foul pole, still shown on highlight reels to this
day.

9. The stakes were high for two of Major League
Baseball's oldest franchises. The Reds hadn't won
a World Series since 1940, and the Red Sox's
Series winless streak dated back all the way to
1918.

10. When it was over, no one wanted it, or the
    baseball season, to end.

This series was certainly not a mismatch on paper,
but Cincinnati had been the best team in baseball all
season and they were expected to win. "The Big Red
Machine," as they were known, had steamrolled the
National League, winning 108 games and clinching a
playoff spot in the first week of September, with a full
month of the season left. They were that good.

Cincinnati had the big names, like the hard-nosed
Pete Rose, who was famous for always giving the
game his all (thus his nickname, "Charlie Hustle");
second-baseman Joe Morgan, who had won the regular season MVP Award (which he would win again
the following season); the brilliant catcher, Johnny
Bench, who had won two MVP Awards of his own
in 1970 and 1972; and the manager with the colorful
nickname, Sparky Anderson.

The Red Sox were good and colorful, too, with two
pitchers, Luis Tiant and Bill Lee, who were as much
showmen and personalities as they were baseball players. Tiant, known as El Tiante, was from Cuba and

when he left his country because of the political climate, he knew he could never return. He was known for his unique pitching delivery on the field and large cigars off of it. Lee was from California, he disliked being told what to do by anyone, would say crazy, funny things, and in general liked to clown around both on the mound and off (earning him the nickname "Spaceman," because his head always seemed to be in outer space), but was such a good pitcher he got away with it all.

The Red Sox earned their ticket to the World Series by toppling the Oakland A's, winner of the previous three World Series, with a three-game sweep in the American League Championship. For Boston to win the World Series for the first time since 1918, they would have to beat two classic teams. They had beaten one in Oakland, but the Big Red Machine was still to come.

The Red Sox looked like they were on their way. Tiant beat a baffled Reds team in the opener in Boston, 6–0. He could throw any pitch from any angle, including a knuckleball. Sometimes when he pitched, Tiant looked up to the sky instead of at home plate while he delivered the ball.

In the second game, with Lee pitching, the Red Sox had the lead once again, up 2–1 in the ninth inning, until the Reds scored two runs and then shut down the Red Sox in the bottom of the ninth. The series headed to Cincinnati tied 1–1.

The Red Sox scored first in Game 3 and would end up hitting three home runs in the game, yet the Reds would overcome the barrage by winning in extra innings, 6–5. The game turned on a controversial call between the Red Sox catcher Carlton Fisk and the Reds pinch-hitter Ed Armbrister, who bunted in the tenth inning, but didn't get out of Fisk's way when Fisk was trying to throw to second base. Fisk took the ball and threw it wildly into center field. The Red Sox screamed and protested that Armbrister interfered, thus forcing the wild throw, and that he should have been called out for interference.

By rule, Armbrister *should* have been called out, but the home plate umpire, Larry Barnett, blew the call. Two batters later, Morgan won the game with a single. The controversy surrounding the non-call seemed to raise the stakes even further.

In Game 4, Tiant showed his toughness. He did not have his best pitches that day, but knew the Red

Sox, down two games to one, could not afford to lose. The game was wild early. The Red Sox led 5–4 after four innings, giving the impression that there would be more runs to score, but there weren't. The final score was 5–4, Red Sox. Most pitchers in baseball today are removed after throwing 100 pitches. On that night, Tiant threw 163, and the Red Sox needed every last one of them.

The series was tied once again.

The Reds won Game 5 by a score of 6–2, putting them a game away from their first championship since 1940. The two teams moved back to Boston for Game 6, with Tiant pitching for the third time, and the Red Sox immediately took a 3–0 lead in the first inning, desperately trying to keep their season alive.

But as the game wore on, the steam in the great pitcher, and in his team, finally ran out. The Reds were just too good. They battered Tiant, who fought bravely against the Cincinnati bats, but was exhausted by a long season, the playoffs, and those 163 pitches he had thrown in Game 4. He had pitched heroically, but the season looked to finally be coming to an end when the Cincinnati center fielder Cesar Geronimo hit a long home run off Tiant in the eighth to make it 6–3.

Then, more magic: Two out, two on, bottom of the eighth, down 6–3, Bernie Carbo entered the game as a pinch hitter for the Red Sox against the Reds' big fireballer, Rawley Eastwick. Eastwick threw so hard that hitters heard the ball pound the catcher's mitt before they saw it.

But somehow, some way, Carbo hit an Eastwick fastball to left center field for a three-run homer.

With one swing of the bat, the game was tied! The Fenway Park fans erupted in cheers.

In the ninth, with Ken Griffey Sr. on first, the dangerous Joe Morgan hit a rocket to right. Dwight Evans, the young Red Sox right fielder, ran all the way back to the wall, 380 feet, and snagged Morgan's drive right by the foul pole. He then turned and threw to first base, beating Griffey back to the bag for a double play.

On to the bottom of the ninth. The Red Sox loaded the bases with no outs! The fans were on their feet, expecting a win. And yet . . . and yet the Sox were unable to score.

Into extra innings went one of the great games of

all time. The Red Sox had been up 3–0, down 6–3, tied 6–6. It was now after midnight, 12:34 a.m. Carlton Fisk was up at bat, facing the eighth Reds pitcher of the game, Pat Darcy. Fisk hit a long fly ball down the left-field line, toward Fenway Park's famous Green Monster, as the giant green wall is known. But would the ball stay fair or go foul? As it soared toward the top of the wall and the foul pole, Fisk could be seen watching it along with everyone else in the stadium. He took a few steps toward first, waving his arms, trying anything and everything to keep the ball fair.

It was. The ball actually hit the foul pole. It was a home run, winning the now-greatest game in World Series history for Red Sox, 7–6.

One more game to decide the series. Winner take all, last game of the baseball season.

The Red Sox, as they had the night before, took a 3–0 lead, this time with Lee on the mound. Yet the Reds were just too good to lose. They fought back, tied the game, and in the ninth inning, Morgan, again, won it with a little bloop single up the middle. The Red Sox had their last chance in the bottom of the ninth, with their future Hall of Famer Yastrzemski at the plate. But Yaz popped up to Geronimo in center. The game was over. The Reds, finally, after losing in 1970 and 1972, were World Series champions.

The Reds and their Big Red Machine had won the best World Series ever, but the real winners were anyone who'd been lucky enough to see it happen.

TOP TEN LIST

The 1975 World Series may always be considered the greatest ever played, but that doesn't mean it stands alone in the debate. Here are ten World Series that were pretty memorable, too.

1. Twins–Braves, 1991: The Twins and Braves both finished in last place the year before, yet they reached the World Series in 1991 and played a seven-game classic.

2. Yankees–Diamondbacks, 2001: Randy Johnson and Curt Schilling combine to win all four games for the D'backs, thwarting the Yankees' bid for a "four-pete" by scoring two runs in the bottom of the ninth of Game 7.

3. Red Sox–Giants, 1912: Three outs from a title, the Giants drop a fly ball and lose!

4. Red Sox–Cardinals, 1946: St. Louis will always

remember Enos Slaughter's dash home all the way from first base!

5. Dodgers–Yankees, 1947: Jackie Robinson's debut World Series . . . Yankees' Bill Bevens loses a no-hitter and the game in the ninth inning of Game 4, Al Giondfriddo robs DiMaggio of a home run in Game 6. Yanks win Game 7!

6. Yankees–Cardinals, 1964: The Rise of the Cardinals. The End of the Yankees Dynasty (for a little while, at least).

7. Cardinals–Royals, 1985: An all-Missouri World Series, a blown call that is still talked about today, lost tempers, and the Royals win their only World Series.

8. Yankees–Giants, 1962: So close, San Francisco, but the Yankees win again!

9. Senators–Giants, 1924: An old-time baseball classic with Game 7 going to extra innings. All-time great Walter Johnson enters the climactic game in relief and earns the win.

10. Cardinals–Tigers, 1934: The famed and colorful Gashouse Gang, huge underdogs to 101-win Detroit, take another World Series for St. Louis.

The Original

REGGIE JACKSON BECOMES MR. OCTOBER

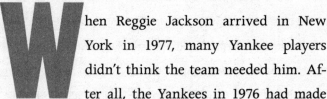

When Reggie Jackson arrived in New York in 1977, many Yankee players didn't think the team needed him. After all, the Yankees in 1976 had made the World Series, and even though they were swept in four painful games by the Big Red Machine that was the Cincinnati Reds, those Yankees had reached the World Series for the first time since 1964. It was the longest stretch a Yankees team had gone without reaching the championship since before Babe Ruth arrived in 1920.

But George Steinbrenner, the fiery, impatient owner of the Yankees, believed his team was missing an important piece. So instead of looking into the draft or a trade, Steinbrenner ventured into a new concept called *free agency* and signed the biggest fish in the game, Reggie Jackson.

Today, everyone is used to players changing teams when their contracts expire, but for one hundred years, baseball contracts *didn't exactly* expire. They automatically renewed each year without the players' consent, and that meant that a baseball player could never change teams by his own choice when his contract was up because, technically, his contract never ended. The only way a player *could* change teams was to be released or traded by the club that had signed him. It was an unfair system and baseball players were totally at the mercy of it. They had one choice: play for the team that signed you, or don't play Major League Baseball at all.

All of that changed in 1975, when MLB was forced by an arbitrator to change its rules. It became illegal for players to be restricted to playing for one team only. After their contracts ended, players were now able to play for any team that wanted them, and after losing the World Series in 1976, Steinbrenner wanted Reggie Jackson.

Reggie Jackson had already been a champion. He was the offensive power of the great Oakland A's teams that won three straight World Series titles from 1972 through 1974. He was a big talker who was completely confident in his ability to play baseball, and he let everyone know it. He was known for being so self-confident that even some of his teammates privately wanted him to fail, just to remind him once in a while to be humble.

Jackson, in so many ways, was the modern-day Babe Ruth: huge in personality, playing in New York, and brought to the city to restore its greatness. The Yankees had never even been to the World Series before Ruth arrived, and similar to the time of Ruth, just before Jackson joined the team, the Yankees hadn't won the World Series in fifteen years.

Jackson immediately made enemies with virtually everyone. There was his enormous contract, the value of which no one in the sport had seen before—four years for $2.5 million. The core of tough, hard-nosed players on the Yankees, such as team captain Thurman

Munson, Graig Nettles, and Lou Piniella, didn't like Jackson's flashy style, didn't think he would fit in, and didn't think the Yankees needed him.

The team's general manager, Gabe Paul, tolerated Jackson because of Steinbrenner, yet the manager, Billy Martin, made it very clear he didn't want Jackson on his team. Martin went so far as ask Yankees management to trade Jackson—something he did more than once. Combined with Jackson's huge personality, it was an explosive mix. Jackson knew people were jealous of his salary, but he didn't care. He understood the power of New York and said outrageous things that somehow came true.

"If I played in New York," Jackson said, "they'd name a candy bar for me."

And they did. The Reggie! bar hit stores in 1977, just like the Baby Ruth had years back.

Jackson and Martin fought right from the beginning, and it didn't help that the Yankees won only two of their first ten games, landing them in last place. Soon enough, though, the Yankees won games, and lots of them—eleven out of their next twelve.

Winning didn't make life easier, though. It certainly didn't help when Jackson gave an interview that insulted Munson, and the two ended up fighting like fifth graders at recess. Jackson also referred to himself in a magazine as "the straw that stirs the drink." This made everyone in the clubhouse mad, because baseball is regarded as a team game, and it appeared that Jackson was putting himself above everyone else.

Things went from bad to worse: the Yankees eventually came back to earth and began losing games. In a particularly bad loss to Boston, Jackson and Martin got into a fight in the dugout on national TV and had to be separated by Yankee players and coaches. Everything was falling apart. Most people who had watched sports had seen periodic fights between teams, but these guys were on the same team!

But Jackson still had his flair for the big stage, just like Babe Ruth, and he hit a game-winning home run in Detroit in the eleventh inning that calmed things down, and the Yankees began soaring again.

The Yankees were winning, holding off Boston and Baltimore during the season, but Jackson had made few friends on the team. Martin and Munson still didn't like him. Even as the team won, Jackson would sometimes think coming to New York had been a big mistake.

The Yankees wound up winning 100 games and the division. Yet winning the division wasn't good enough. Only one thing, Jackson knew, would make all the negativity go away: coming up big in the playoffs.

The Yankees beat Kansas City in the American League Championship and were back in the World Series, this time facing their old rivals, the Dodgers. After five games, the Yankees led three games to two and headed home to New York with a chance to win the World Series for the first time since 1962. All of New York was watching. And after a season of talk and turmoil, all of New York was watching Reggie.

In the fourth inning of Game 6, with a runner on, Jackson launched Burt Hooton's first pitch for a two-run home run, giving the Yankees the lead.

In the fifth inning, Jackson came up again, this time against Elias Sosa.

Sosa threw one pitch.

Jackson hit that pitch for another two-run home run. The Yankees led 7–3.

The next time Jackson came up, it was against Charlie Hough, the knuckleballer.

Hough threw one pitch.

Jackson hit it 450 feet to the moon, over the center field wall for another home run.

It was like something out of a movie. The fans were going crazy, shouting "REG-GIE! REG-GIE!" Jackson came out of the dugout and gave a curtain call, as if he were an actor on stage. Then he looked into the television camera and put up three fingers.

Three pitchers.

Three pitches.

Three home runs.

And the Yankees won the World Series.

Only one other man had ever hit three home runs in a World Series game—of course, it was the man in whose footsteps Jackson followed, the man who, like Jackson, had been a star and a champion before but made himself a legend in New York—none other than the legendary Babe Ruth.

Jackson was the first player ever to score ten runs in a World Series. He wound up hitting .450, with five home runs in the six-game series. For everyone who disliked him during the season, for everyone who was mad at him for his big talk, he had won them over.

Jackson had conquered New York and more. He'd made good on all of his crazy promises. Because of Jackson, New York was once again the center of the baseball world. The city had something it hadn't had since Babe Ruth: a larger-than-life star on the field and off who did his loudest talking with his bat.

He was also given a new nickname: Mr. October.

Reggie did something else, too: he created a blueprint that every future big-money player, acquired either by trade or free agency, from Dave Winfield to Rickey Henderson to Carlos Beltran to Alex Rodriguez, would try to do—come to the big city and deliver a championship.

"I didn't come to New York to be a star," Jackson said. "I brought my star with me." They say it isn't bragging if you can do it, and nobody backed up big talk like Reggie Jackson, *Mr. October,* that night in 1977.

TOP TEN LIST

Reggie Jackson's three-homer game in Game 6 of the 1977 World Series revived the Yankees name and made Reggie a New York icon. In a sport full of them, here are ten more iconic and infamous World Series moments.

1. 1954, Game 1: Willie Mays of the New York Giants robs Vic Wertz with an unbelievable catch in center field.

2. 1975, Game 6: Boston's Carlton Fisk hits a twelfth-inning home run to beat Cincinnati and force a deciding Game 7.

3. 1932, Game 3: Fifth inning, Babe Ruth's "called shot." He pointed to the outfield and then hit a home run to the exact spot.

4. 1988, Game 1: Bottom of the ninth, two out, Dodgers down a run to the A's. An injured Kirk Gibson hits a game-winning, pinch-hit homer to beat Oakland, then limps around the bases.

5. 1956, Game 1: Jackie Robinson steals home against the Yankees.

6. 2011, Game 3: St. Louis's Albert Pujols hits three home runs against Texas.

7. 1968, Game 1: Bob Gibson is dominant, striking out 17 against Detroit.

8. 1956, Game 5: Yankees' Don Larsen throws the only perfect game in World Series history.

9. 2012, Game 1: Pablo Sandoval hits three home runs. Giants beat the Tigers.

10. 1986, Game 6: Red Sox–Mets: With the Sox one out away from winning the championship, Mookie Wilson's ground ball goes between Bill Buckner's legs for an error! The Mets go on to win the series.

"Don't Give Us a Chance"

THE 2004 BOSTON RED SOX

To win a best-of-seven playoff series, one team has to win four games. By midnight after Game 3 of the 2004 American League Championship Series, when the New York Yankees demolished the Boston Red Sox 19–8 to take a 3–0 lead and climb one win away from going to the World Series for the second year in a row, no one in Boston would have minded if they just skipped the fourth game. Maybe no one in Boston would have cared if baseball had never been played again, ever.

For Red Sox fans, it was all too much: too much pain and not enough victory. The people of Boston were fiercely loyal to their beloved Red Sox—there was so much caring about the team, so many years of winning only to lose at the end, and often in the worst possible ways. Too many years invested, every summer of sun and hope and fun for as long as anyone could remember only to end in heartbreak. The worst part was that so much of the losing was to the same team: the hated Yankees.

They liked to call it a "rivalry," but was it really? A rivalry is when one team wins one year, and the other wins the next. This Yankees–Red Sox relationship was more like the hammer and the nail—a whole lot of hurt in Boston at the hands of New York.

What was the point of continuing? The result was always going to be the same, because it hadn't changed in more than a century. Even during years when the Red Sox were great, the Yankees were better. The Red Sox just couldn't find a way to beat them. It wasn't that the people of Boston stopped caring—it was that they cared too much only to have their hearts broken.

Fans had to go back—*way* back!—to a time before their parents and grandparents were born to remember when it wasn't this way. The Yankees had beaten the Red Sox when Boston traded a pitcher named Babe Ruth to New York in 1920, and not only did he become the greatest player of all time, but the Yankees became the greatest *team* of all time. Before the Ruth trade, the Red Sox had won five of the first fifteen World Series. The Yankees never even *reached* the series until Ruth arrived.

Then, from 1919 to 2003, the Yankees won twenty-six World Series. The Red Sox won zero.

When the Red Sox won 96 games in 1949, the Yankees won 97 and went to the series. The Sox would win 94 games the following season . . . but of course the Yankees won 98 games and again went to the series. In 1978 the Red Sox had a 14-game lead over the Yankees with two months left in the season. The Yankees would go on to tie Boston in the regular season and then beat the Sox in a one-game playoff to decide the division winner. The Red Sox went home, heartbroken, while the Yankees went on to win the World Series.

In 1994 Major League Baseball changed its playoff format. For the first time, a wild card team that failed to win its division would qualify for the play-offs. In the first five years of the wild card format, the Yankees and Red Sox claimed four of the five slots in the American League. This gave the two teams a chance to meet in the playoffs. It finally happened in 1999 when they met in the American League Championship Series. The result? The Yankees won in five games and went on to win the World Series.

The Yankees and Red Sox would go on to meet once more with the World Series on the line, in 2003. Despite finishing second to the Yankees in the American League East Division, the Red Sox believed they had the better team. This was to be a classic American League Championship Series. It went to seven games and only ended when the Yankees' Aaron Boone hit a series-winning home run in the bottom of the eleventh inning, leading the Yankees to yet another World Series.

The 2004 Red Sox team was supposed to be different. They had to wait an entire year for the opportunity to get revenge. Now, here they were, exactly where they had envisioned themselves—playing the

Yankees for another chance to get to the World Series. Yet they were now down 3 games to 0. No one gave them much chance to come all the way back and win.

For some reason, hours before Game 4 the next afternoon, near the home dugout at Fenway Park, Red Sox first baseman Kevin Millar was in a surprisingly great mood. "All I'm going to say is, don't give us a chance," Millar said. "If they're going to beat us, they better beat us tonight, because in Game 5, we've got Pedro going, and if we get that game, then we go back to New York. If we go back to New York, then all the pressure is on them, because they'll know they *have* to win. If we go back to New York, that's bad enough for them, because it's not supposed to go back there. And if it gets to a Game 7, no way will we lose."

Millar walked away. Meanwhile, Red Sox officials were talking about how the game was sold out but many people were trying to sell their tickets and were even having trouble doing that, because no Red Sox fan wanted to witness losing yet again to the Yankees.

The Yankees had Orlando Hernandez on the mound. Hernandez was one of the great playoff pitchers of his time. He had eleven postseason decisions and had won nine of them. The Yankees were in a good position.

New York jumped out to a 2–0 lead when Alex Rodriguez, considered the best player in all of baseball at the time, hit a two-run homer off of Derek Lowe in the third inning. Before the season had even begun, the Red Sox and Yankees had competed in a bidding war to acquire Rodriguez from the Texas Rangers. The Red Sox thought they had struck a deal with Texas, but then, at the last second, the deal was nullified. The Yankees swooped in, traded for Rodriguez and, in a different sort of contest, beat the Red Sox yet again.

Even down 2–0 thanks to Rodriguez, the Red Sox were far from ready to call it quits. Boston chased El Duque by scoring three two-out runs in the fifth, including a go-ahead two-run single by David Ortiz. But in the next inning, the Yankees took the lead right back with two runs and led 4–3.

It stayed that way until the bottom of the ninth. Three more outs and Boston would be finished. Another year, another gut-wrenching loss to the Yankees. Mariano Rivera, the great Yankees closer, the greatest closer to ever play, was on the mound. He had shut the Red Sox down in the eighth and now faced Millar to start the ninth.

Then things began to change. Millar worked a walk, and was replaced by pinch-runner Dave Roberts, a speedy backup outfielder who had been acquired from San Diego late in the season. Roberts had one job: to steal second. When he took off, it looked like he would be caught. The throw by the catcher, Jorge Posada, beat Roberts . . . but he slipped in just under Derek Jeter's glove: safe!

The next batter, Bill Mueller, the Red Sox's third baseman, stepped to the plate and singled up the middle. Roberts came home to score and the game was tied, 4–4!

The Red Sox looked about to win the game right there. Mueller went to second on a bunt and then to third on an error, but Rivera regrouped and escaped without further damage.

The two teams went to extra innings. They remained tied until the twelfth inning, when David "Big Papi" Ortiz homered off Paul Quantrill, giving the Red Sox a 6–4 victory.

A great win, but still, winning Game 4 was just one game. The Red Sox could not lose again. They couldn't afford any big mistakes or they would be going home. The great Pedro Martinez, maybe the greatest pitcher of his time, pitched Game 5 for Boston, while the excellent Mike Mussina pitched for the Yankees.

The Red Sox quickly scored two in the first, but the Yankees remained unfazed and came back to score four runs off Martinez, including three in the sixth inning, giving them a 4–2 lead.

But momentum began to shift the Red Sox's way. Martinez had lost the lead, but with two on and two out in the sixth, Boston right fielder Trot Nixon snared a sinking line drive by Hideki Matsui that would have scored at least two more runs. Nixon's catch kept the game within reach.

After a long season and the grueling extra-innings game the night before, the Yankees' bullpen was weary. Nixon's catch in the sixth inning grew even more important when Ortiz, who had won Game 4, hit another home run in the eighth to make it 4–3, cutting the Yankees' lead to just one run. As the pressure mounted, Yankee pitcher Tom "Flash" Gordon walked Kevin Millar and gave up a single to Nixon, putting the speedy Dave Roberts at third base.

Yankee manager Joe Torre turned once again to the great Rivera, giving him a second chance to close out the series. But it turned out to be déjà vu for Rivera, who gave up a fly ball to Jason Varitek that scored Roberts, and the Red Sox and Yankees were tied again.

Then some good luck went Boston's way: In the top of the ninth, with Ruben Sierra on first base, Yankees first baseman Tony Clark hit a double down the right field line. The ball hit the dirt and bounced on one hop into the stands for a ground-rule double. Had the ball stayed low and bounced around the outfield wall, Sierra would have had an excellent chance to score from first and the Yankees would have had the lead again, but it was not to be. Boston escaped the inning without allowing a run.

As yet another game went to extra innings, nerves frayed and the players wearied. Boston and New York remained tied until late into the night. Then, in the fourteenth inning, Ortiz—who had won Game 4 with a home run and kept the Red Sox alive in this game with a homer in the eighth—hit a single up the middle off of Esteban Loaiza to score Johnny Damon.

The Red Sox, whom no one in Boston wanted to see lose, had won again!

This wasn't happening, was it?

It was.

The Red Sox were still alive and going back to New York for the final two games of the series.

Kevin Millar turned out to be right: When the Red Sox returned to New York for the final two games, they destroyed the Yankees. Curt Schilling, pitching on an injured left ankle that was so bad he bled through his sock, shut the Yankees out early while the Red Sox took a 4–0 lead and held on to win Game 6, 4–2, setting up a winner-takes-all Game 7 at Yankee Stadium, the same place where the Red Sox had lost a year before.

This time, there would be no suspense. The Yankees were tired and beaten while the Red Sox soared. Ortiz (again!) hit a home run in the first inning. Damon hit a grand slam in the second and it was 6–0 before many of the 56,129 fans expecting a Yankee win had even gotten to their seats.

The final score was 10–3, Boston. It was the greatest comeback in the history of baseball. No team had ever come back from being down three games to none to win a playoff series. For eighty-six years the Red Sox had found a way to lose to the Yankees, but in 2004, in the most improbable of ways, Boston finally beat the team that had brought them so much pain.

The World Series went by fast. The Red Sox demolished the St. Louis Cardinals in four straight games to win the World Series for the first time since 1918. The losing was over. The Red Sox had become champions by coming back from three games down and not losing again for the rest of the season.

From that day since, Red Sox history changed. The Red Sox would no longer be expected to lose, but to win. Ortiz grew into the symbol of victory in Boston, not another player just good enough to lose to the Yankees. Boston would win the World Series again in 2007 and 2013. The magic the Yankees held over them for all those decades would disappear and the two teams would finally be what they were supposed to be: true rivals once and for all.

"I'm going to say two things," David Ortiz said

in 2014. "The first is I have no idea why Millar was so positive. I thought he was crazy. No one was saying 'We're going to lose' in the clubhouse, but being down that much to the Yankees, well, you knew that something amazing had to happen.

"The second thing," Ortiz said, "is that I completely forgot we were down *three games to none*! I thought it was three games to one. To come all the way back like that? Three games to none? Against the Yankees? I don't think you're ever gonna see that again."

The 2004 Boston Red Sox

TOP TEN LIST

People around Boston will never forget 2004, when the Red Sox won for the first time in 86 years, but other cities have their defining championship moments, too.

1. Chicago White Sox 2005: First championship in eighty-eight years.
2. Brooklyn Dodgers 1955: Only championship in Brooklyn's history.
3. San Francisco Giants 2010: First ever World Series for San Francsico.
4. Toronto Blue Jays 1992: First Canadian team to win a World Series.
5. Kansas City Royals 1985: First and only title for the Royals.
6. Cincinnati Reds 1975: First World Series win since 1940.

7. Milwaukee Braves 1957: Only baseball championship in Milwaukee to this day.

8. Pittsburgh Pirates 1960: First title in Pittsburgh since 1925.

9. New York Yankees 1977: The Yankee Dynasty returns.

10. Philadelphia Phillies 1980: Founded in 1883, the Phillies finally win!

Joy and Heartbreak

THE 2011 WORLD SERIES

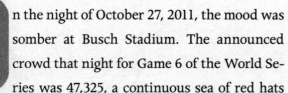n the night of October 27, 2011, the mood was somber at Busch Stadium. The announced crowd that night for Game 6 of the World Series was 47,325, a continuous sea of red hats and windbreakers, white St. Louis Cardinals home replica jerseys underneath. St. Louis is as passionately and deeply committed to its baseball team as any city in America. Even after the Cardinals' opponent, the Texas Rangers, had piled on run after run all game long, taking a sizable lead into the late innings, thousands of loyal Cardinals fans were prepared to cheer for their team, to congratulate them on a great sea-

son even though it was the Rangers who were just moments away from winning their first-ever World Series.

The Rangers had been here before. A year earlier, they had reached the World Series for the first time in their 38-year history. They beat the vaunted New York Yankees in the American League Championship Series four games to two, and were pitted against the San Francisco Giants, another team that had never won the World Series, not since leaving New York for the Bay Area in 1958. Texas had been heavily favored because of their great offensive lineup—including the dynamic American League MVP Josh Hamilton, all-time franchise hits leader Michael Young, the always-dangerous Vladimir Guerrero, and the young power-hitting outfielder Nelson Cruz. Yet the Giants' superior pitching surprised the mighty Rangers in stunning fashion, helping San Francisco to win the championship in five easy games. The Rangers had enjoyed a magical year and losing was hard, but the team that had always lived in the shadow of the Dallas Cowboys was becoming a baseball power.

They returned in 2011 as fully loaded as ever, losing the aging Guerrero but adding all-star third base-man Adrian Beltre, who could do it all: hit for power, hit for average, and play the field with Gold Glove defense. They had six all-stars in 2011 and wound up running away with the division, winning it by ten games.

And then there were the 2011 Cardinals, a team that wasn't even supposed to make the playoffs. They had been so far out of a playoff spot as the calendar turned to September—10 1/2 games—that the possibility of making the World Series wasn't even a thought in the minds of the Cardinals' faithful.

But then two things happened simultaneously: First, the Cardinals just kept fighting. In fact, they went 23–9 to finish the season, easily their hottest stretch of the year. Second, the Atlanta Braves just kept losing, suffering one of the greatest collapses in the history of the game. The Braves blew that 10 1/2-game lead and capped it off by losing on the final day of the season to give the Cardinals a last-minute postseason berth.

St. Louis then slipped by Philadelphia in the National League Division Series, beating the 102-win Phillies 1–0 in Philadelphia in a classic Game 5 series finale. Then, in the National League Championship Series, the Cards went on to beat Milwaukee in six games. Somehow the team that wasn't even in the playoff race as late as September had reached the World Series.

The powerhouse Rangers, hungry to complete what they had begun the season before, had defeated the Tigers in the American League Championship Series and now awaited the Cardinals.

The Rangers may have fielded a lineup full of big hitters, but the Cardinals had a couple of stars of their own, including a legend at first base, Albert Pujols. Pujols had won the National League Most Valuable Player Award *three* times! He had also already won a World Series title with the Cardinals, back in 2006. He was clearly on a path that would lead to the Hall of Fame one day.

Yet his biggest moment was still to come. It occurred in Game 3, when he forever etched his name in the World Series record books by hitting three home runs. Only two players had ever done that before, and they were two of the biggest names ever: Babe Ruth and Reggie Jackson.

Pujols provided a legendary moment on the biggest

stage, propelling the Cardinals to a two-games-to-one lead. But mighty Texas rebounded quickly, going on to win the next two games at home to gain a 3–2 lead.

The series returned to St. Louis with the Rangers one game away from their first World Series championship. They could practically taste the victory.

Game Six . . . Game Six . . . Game Six! . . . So many emotions running through the fans of both teams. At first, the game was close, but when back-to-back home runs from Beltre and Cruz helped the Rangers take a 7–4 lead after seven innings, it was looking like a Texas victory parade was imminent.

Yet, as they had already proven that season, the Cardinals weren't a team to give up easily. And they knew that their three-run deficit could have easily been more. Texas had missed a couple of opportunities to score even *more* runs. So even though they were two innings away from losing the World Series, the Cardinals had hope. And hope is a powerful thing.

They began by scoring once in the bottom of the eighth inning. Now they were down by just two runs. Which was great, except . . . now the Rangers were just three outs away from winning the championship with a two-run lead. Every Ranger on the field and in the dugout could practically feel the win in their hands.

The top of the ninth was a quiet one for Texas. Their lead would remain two runs headed to the bottom of the ninth. Neftali Feliz entered the game to pitch for Texas. Feliz was the Rangers' fireballing closer, the pitcher who came into the game and finished the job. The year before, Feliz had won the Jackie Robinson Award as the American League Rookie of the Year with 40 saves. Thirty-two times in 2011, Feliz entered the game with a lead and walked away with a save. Now, the biggest one of his career was three outs away.

Backup infielder Ryan Theriot was the first batter. Feliz handled him easily. Theriot struck out swinging.

One out.

The next batter was the dangerous Pujols. Pujols wasted no time and swung at the first pitch, rocketing a double to center. Feliz began to fret, so much so that he walked the next batter, veteran outfielder Lance Berkman.

The next batter was the young and talented Allen

Craig, who had hit a home run his last time at bat. It took Feliz six pitches, but he regained control. On that sixth pitch, Craig swung and missed, striking out.

Two outs! Every Ranger stood by the top step of the dugout, eager to run onto the field in celebration.

Third baseman David Freese was up next. David Freese had grown up in nearby Wildwood, right next to St. Louis. He'd been a Cardinals fan his whole life and was now playing in the World Series for his boyhood team. Freese had already won the NLCS MVP Award, hitting .545 against Milwaukee.

None of that mattered now. What mattered was keeping the Cardinals' season alive. What mattered now was doing something, anything, to get on base, because making an out meant the season was over.

Feliz was throwing ninety-six miles an hour. He got ahead of Freese, one ball, two strikes. The Rangers were *one strike* away from being champions. Feliz looked to his catcher for the sign.

He threw a fastball.

Freese connected, hitting a hard shot out to right field. The right fielder, Nelson Cruz, stepped forward, then back . . . and back . . . and then he jumped, his glove out in the air. At first the fans couldn't tell if he had caught the ball or not. He hadn't! The ball bounced off the wall just out of Cruz's reach and ricocheted back into the outfield.

Pujols scored!

Berkman scored!

Freese slid into third base with a triple. The game was tied 7–7 and the St. Louis fans were going crazy!

Feliz tried to regroup, knowing that a single mistake—a wild pitch, a passed ball, a hit—would give the game to the Cardinals.

And to his credit, regroup he did. Right after Freese's triple, the great Cardinals catcher, Yadier Molina, lined out to right field. The inning was over. Feliz walked to the dugout, tears in his eyes.

The two teams would play extra innings.

The Rangers were devastated but not defeated. With one out in the top of the tenth, Elvis Andrus singled and Josh Hamilton, the powerful center fielder, followed by homering to right center. The Rangers once again had the lead, 9–7!

To the bottom of the tenth, the Rangers *again* three outs away from winning the World Series. Darren

Oliver, the Rangers' soft-throwing left-hander, replaced Feliz. The Cardinals again were down to their last three outs, again down by two runs.

This time, the bottom, weaker part of the order was up, but the first two batters singled. Scott Feldman replaced Oliver as pitcher and got the next batter out. It was Theriot's turn again. Would he get a hit? No, he grounded out to third, but a run scored on the play, making it 9–8. The Cardinals were again down to their final out.

And this time Albert Pujols was up. The Rangers weren't taking any chances with Pujols. They walked him intentionally.

Lance Berkman was next. The count went to 2–2.

The Rangers, for the second time this game, were one strike away from the championship.

And for the second time this game, the Cardinals refused to lose. Berkman singled to center to tie the game 9–9!

The Rangers didn't score in the top of the eleventh.

David Freese, who had kept the season alive in the ninth, led off the bottom of the inning for St. Louis.

Mark Lowe was the new Texas pitcher.

Lowe and Freese battled to a full count, three balls and two strikes. With the pressure on, one swing of the bat away from ending the game, David Freese did it again. He hit Lowe's next pitch over the wall for a home run!

Game over. The Cardinals would live to play another game. And David Freese had become a legend in his own time.

The Cardinals and Rangers would play Game 7, the final match to decide the championship.

The next night proved to be fairly anticlimactic. The Rangers managed to score a run in the first inning, but their energy was clearly spent from the heartbreak of the night before. The Cardinals, on the other hand, coming off an improbable comeback win, were soaring at home, so close to a championship that back in September never seemed possible. The Cardinals won Game 7 with ease. The final score was 6–2.

In the Rangers clubhouse, few players had anything to say, for no words could make up for being so close to a championship only to lose in such a heartbreaking manner. There were teams, like the 1986

Red Sox, that had been a strike away from winning the World Series, but no team in baseball history had ever been one strike away twice.

The photos of the 2011 series, as with so many other championships, focus on the winners—photos of World Series MVP David Freese and Yadier Molina leaping up in the air, and their frenzied fans doing the same, enjoying the happiest moments of their lives. The other side of those emotions, of the Rangers defeated and deflated, pained and drained by the competition and the losing, is for a time the loneliest feeling in the world.

Their manager, Ron Washington, would feel the hurt of losing the World Series for years to come. After the game, he immediately congratulated the Cardinals for their victory, before returning to his office and uttering these words: "This is competition. It's why we play. We lost today, but we'll keep fighting and fighting until one day we win. That's baseball."

TOP TEN LIST

The Texas Rangers didn't win the World Series in 2010 or in 2011, but by appearing in back-to-back World Series, the Rangers made Texas, better known for its football, pay attention to baseball as well. Here are ten teams that didn't always win, but deserve to remain in the hearts of their fans.

1. Brooklyn Dodgers 1947–55: Jackie Robinson and the Boys of Summer.
2. Kansas City Royals 2014: After twenty losing seasons and no playoff appearances between 1986 and 2013, the Royals made an unlikely World Series run and, despite losing the decisive Game 7 to the Giants by one run, the team brought winning baseball back to Kansas City.
3. Seattle Mariners 1995–2001: This group never

reached the World Series, but they did win three division titles and a wild card playoff led by Ken Griffey Jr., Edgar Martinez, a young Alex Rodriguez, and pitcher Randy Johnson.

4. Cleveland Indians 1995–2001: This group led by stars such as Manny Ramirez, Albert Belle, Jim Thome, and Roberto Alomar reached the World Series in 1995 and 1997, but lost both.

5. Atlanta Braves 1991–2005: *Fourteen consecutive* division titles! They were led by the greatest pitching staff of all time, featuring future Hall-of-Famers Greg Maddux and Tom Glavine.

6. Boston Red Sox 1974–1978: Lot of heartbreak in Boston, but the Sox had Carl "Yaz" Yastrzemski, Jim Rice, Carlton Fisk, Luis Tiant, and the most exciting World Series in history.

7. San Francisco Giants 1960–1969: Willie Mays, Willie McCovey, Orlando Cepeda, Gaylord Perry, and Juan Marichal—five Hall of Famers!

8. Oakland A's 1987–1992: Jose Canseco, Mark McGwire, Rickey Henderson, Dennis Eckersly, and Dave Stewart. Three World Series appearances, one win.

9. Milwaukee Brewers 1978–1983: Nicknamed "Harvey's Wallbangers" for their ability to hit home runs, they were the first and only Brewers team to reach the World Series, in 1982. Rollie Fingers, Robin Yount, and Paul Molitor were all inducted into the Hall of Fame.

10. Houston Astros 1997–2005: The "Killer B's" of Jeff Bagwell, Craig Biggio, and Lance Berkman starred for this group. The 'Stros won consecutive division titles in 1997, 1998, and 1999 before finally reaching the World Series in 2005 (losing to the White Sox).

Babe Ruth wears his crown. (1921)

Jackie Robinson on the set of The Jackie Robinson Story. *(1950)*

Willie Mays's "The Catch." (1954)

Charles M. Schulz, creator of the legendary Peanuts *comic strip, pays homage to Willie Mays. (1966)*

Sandy Koufax pitches for the Los Angeles Dodgers in Game 7 of the 1965 World Series.

Hank Aaron at a press conference after breaking the all-time home run record. (1974)

Rickey Henderson breaks the career stolen bases record. (1991)

Boston Braves second baseman Johnny Evers and manager George Stallings in the dugout. (1914)

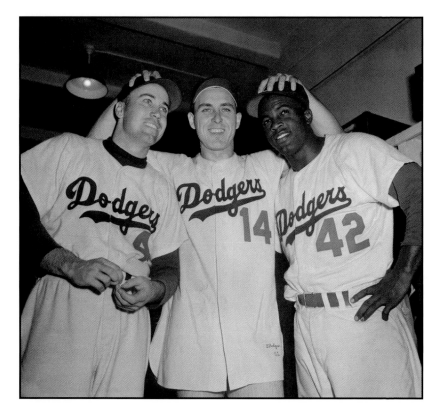

Jackie Robinson with Gil Hodges and Duke Snider. (1952)

Owner Charlie Finley with the 1974 Oakland A's.

Barry Bonds with manager Dusty Baker. (1993)

Mark McGwire and Sammy Sosa share a hug. (1998)

New York's Daily News *celebrates the local champs. (1998)*

*Bill Mazeroski helps the Pittsburgh Pirates win the 1960
World Series with a walk-off home run.*

Roberto Clemente slides into home plate. (1969)

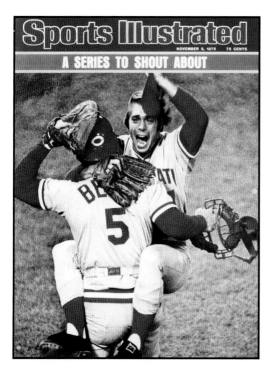

Will McEnaney and Johnny Bench celebrate the Cincinnati Reds' 1975 World Series victory over the Boston Red Sox.

Reggie Jackson reaches out to his fans. (1977)

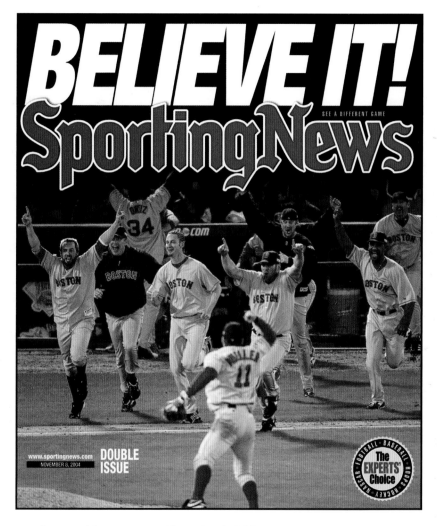

Sporting News *cover on November 8, 2004, celebrating*
the Boston Red Sox's return to glory.

The St. Louis Cardinals celebrate their 2011 World Series victory over a heartbroken Texas Rangers team.

A Timeline of Baseball's Key Moments (Top 40 Style)

1. 1869: The Cincinnati Red Stockings become baseball's first professional team
2. 1884: Pitchers were allowed to throw overhand
3. 1903: Boston defeats Pittsburgh in the first "World Series"
4. 1908: The Chicago Cubs win the World Series for the last time (so far)
5. 1920: The ball is changed to a "live" ball for more offense
6. 1927: Babe Ruth hits 60 home runs in a single season
7. 1933: The first All-Star Game is played
8. 1935: Babe Ruth retires with 714 home runs
9. 1939: The National Baseball Hall of Fame and Museum opens

10. 1939: Lou Gehrig plays the last of a record 2,130 consecutive games

11. 1941: Ted Williams hits .406, the last player to hit .400

12. 1941: Joe DiMaggio sets the consecutive-games hitting streak record with 56 in a row

13. 1947: Jackie Robinson becomes the first African American player in the major leagues

14. 1947: Larry Doby becomes the American League's first African American player

15. 1951: Major League Baseball's first transcontinental TV broadcast

16. 1958: The Brooklyn Dodgers and New York Giants move to Los Angeles and San Francisco

17. 1961: Roger Maris hits 61 home runs, breaking Babe Ruth's single-season record

18. 1969: The American and National Leagues each split into two divisions

19. 1969: The pitcher's mound is lowered from fifteen inches to ten, again to help the offense

20. 1972: Hank Aaron signs the richest contract in history at the time: three years, $600,000

21. 1973: The American League adopts the designated hitter rule

22. 1974: Hank Aaron breaks Babe Ruth's all-time home run record

23. 1974: Catfish Hunter signs five-year, $3.75 million contract with the Yankees

24. 1975: The Cleveland Indians name Frank Robinson the first African American manager

25. 1975: Players granted free agency by arbitrator Peter Seitz

26. 1981: Players strike for fifty days

27. 1987: The Chicago Cubs play Wrigley Field's first-ever night game

28. 1994: Players strike on August 12; World Series cancelled for first time since 1904

29. 1995: Major League Baseball introduces wild card playoff teams

30. 1995: Cal Ripken Jr. breaks Lou Gehrig's consecutive games played streak

31. 1997: Major League Baseball introduces interleague play

32. 1997: The Florida Marlins become the first wild-card team to win the World Series

33. 1998: Mark McGwire hits 70 home runs, breaking Roger Maris's single-season record

34. 2000: Alex Rodriguez signs a ten-year, $252

million contract with the Texas Rangers

35. 2001: Barry Bonds hits 73 home runs, breaking Mark McGwire's single-season record

36. 2004: The Boston Red Sox win the World Series for the first time since 1918

37. 2005: The Chicago White Sox win the World Series for the first time since 1917

38. 2007: Barry Bonds breaks Hank Aaron's all-time home run record, finishing his career with 762

39. 2010: The San Francisco Giants win the World Series for the first time

40. 2014: Major League Baseball introduces instant replay challenge system

INDEX